DINNER FOR A FIVER

D0357948

DINNER FOR A FIVER

Over 150 best-value recipes from
Britain's top restaurants

NICHOLAS LANDER
with Jancis Robinson

VERMILION
LONDON

For Jancis, whom I love, and
for Julia, William and Rose, whom I live for.

First published 1994
1 3 5 7 9 10 8 6 4 2

Nicholas Lander has asserted his right under the Copyright, Designs and Patents Act,
1988 to be identified as the author of this work.

All rights reserved. No part of this publication may be reproduced, stored in a
retrieval system, or transmitted in any form or by any means, electronic,
mechanical, photocopying, recording or otherwise, without the prior permission of
the copyright owner.

First published in the United Kingdom in 1994 by Vermilion
an imprint of Ebury Press
Random House UK Ltd, 20 Vauxhall Bridge Road,
London SW1V 2SA

Random House Australia (Pty) Limited
20 Alfred Street, Milsons Point, Sydney
New South Wales 2061, Australia

Random House New Zealand Limited
18 Poland Road, Glenfield
Auckland 10, New Zealand

Random House South Africa (Pty) Limited
PO Box 337, Bergvlei, South Africa

Random House UK Limited Reg. No. 9540009

A CIP catalogue record for this book is available from
the British Library

ISBN 0 09 178309 7

Illustrations by Kim Dalziel

Typeset in Century Old Style by Textype Typesetters, Cambridge
Printed and bound in Great Britain by Cox & Wyman Ltd

Papers used by Ebury Press are
natural recyclable products made
from wood grown in sustainable forests.

CONTENTS

Acknowledgements

I owe enormous thanks to: my sister, Katie, whose idea this book was, to all those at the *Financial Times*, who supported 'Lunch for a Fiver' and this book, to Caradoc King, to Rowena Webb, a listening editor, to Kim Dalziel, and to Barbara Croxford for being ultra professional. Most importantly, to all the chefs and restaurateurs who put up with my nagging letters and phone calls. And, of course, to Jancis, without whose help I would never have written my first article.

Part One

THE ORIGINS OF 'DINNER FOR A FIVER'

This book is based on a restaurant promotion which I launched in the *Financial Times* on Saturday, January 2, 1993. The promotion was called 'Lunch for a Fiver' and it brought together 130 restaurants around Great Britain who, for a fortnight at the end of January, offered a two-course lunch for £5, inclusive of VAT.

'Lunch for a Fiver' was a huge success. It proved to be far more popular than I had dreamt of or even dared to anticipate when, during the last three months of 1992, I spent my entire time writing letters and faxes, phoning and cajoling sceptical restaurateurs into participating.

'Lunch for a Fiver' filled all the participating restaurants during what is traditionally the quietest period of their year, and brought back to many restaurateurs fond memories of the mid-1980s when all restaurants had seemed to be busy – and sold extra copies of the *Financial Times*.

One sign of its success was that the promotion was continued by many of those who had taken part. Even in early July, five months later, a number of restaurants were carrying on with their own particular 'Lunch for a Fiver', and many more had realised that to fill tables and please customers they had to offer good food and good value, all wrapped up in a good-looking deal.

It also won praise from other food and restaurant writers. The *Guardian*, *Time Out* and the *Observer* all praised it warmly while one writer from *The Times* crossed a crowded room in a West End hotel to, as he put it, 'pay homage to the man who thought of Lunch for a Fiver' (journalists can be extremely sarcastic!) And, if imitation is the sincerest form of flattery, then the actions of two other newspapers which came out with their own version of 'Lunch for a Fiver' within days of the *FT* campaign ending can only be construed as very high praise indeed.

It brought me a sackful of letters from readers and diners. Not all were entirely laudatory and there was particular venom reserved for one restaurateur who, in his two London restaurants, imposed a mandatory cover charge of £1.70 on every meal. Many wrote in to say that the scheme had made them think again about going out to restaurants after rising prices had forced them to give up this otherwise most pleasurable habit. It also brought the restaurant industry badly needed new customers. One letter came from the parent of a seventeen-year-old boy who had, thanks to 'Lunch for a Fiver', been able to take his girlfriend out to a proper restaurant for the first time.

And, fulfilling Andy Warhol's prophecy, it brought me fifteen minutes' fame, including brief appearances on television, radio and in various newspapers, all of which were enjoyable. The most surprising report has to be an article on 'Lunch for a Fiver' which appeared in *Propaganda,* a Brazilian marketing magazine, naturally enough in Portuguese.

I would be the first to admit that the success of 'Lunch for a Fiver' owed a great deal to timing – Great Britain in early January 1993 with no end to the recession in sight was not a happy place – good luck and the unequivocal backing of the senior management at the *Financial Times* who allowed me to put the scheme together without any interference.

But there was one other magic ingredient which links the success of those restaurateurs who participated wholeheartedly in 'Lunch for a Fiver', with what you can do with their recipes in your own kitchen.

You require many essential characteristics to be a successful restaurateur. You have to be an eternal optimist; to have a certain amount of good taste, at least as far as food and wine are concerned; to be prepared to spend most of your long working day on your feet in what can be very warm conditions; and, should the worst eventualities happen and the washer-up fail to show, to lead by example and do the washing up yourself.

But there is one other essential ingredient which I believe during the late 1980s and early 1990s many restaurateurs chose to ignore. To be a good restaurateur you have to have a generous disposition. You must want to care for and look after your customers. In short, to take an interest in your fellow man.

Possibly as an ex-restaurateur I am acutely aware of this, but this prevailing lack of generosity became only too obvious in many of the replies I received to my introductory letter. Too many said that they did not need the scheme, seemingly not stopping to consider whether their customers did. One 'leading' London restaurateur replied that not only did he not need 'Lunch for a Fiver' but in his opinion it would lead to financial ruin for all those taking part.

What 'Lunch for a Fiver' did was not only offer unbeatable value but also prove to a general public that had grown increasingly sceptical as the cost of eating out in this country had gone up – often losing touch with the quality on offer – that there is a large number of restaurateurs who *do* care about their customers and who were prepared to make the short term financial sacrifice that 'Lunch for a Fiver' entailed to make this apparent.

This spirit of generosity applies equally when you are entertaining at home. Preparing a dinner party or cooking lunch for friends at home over the weekend is not easy. You have to think about the menu, work your way around the suppliers, or the various aisles of the supermarket, carry it all home and unload it. And all that before you have started cooking.

Then there is the cooking itself, which can take you away from your guests and their conversation – after all the whole point of inviting them over – to be followed by the clearing away and the washing up (possibly the biggest difference between eating at home and in a restaurant).

But when it does go well – the recipes work, the wine is good and the conversation stimulating – cooking for friends around your dinner table can be a wonderful experience, well worth the effort and the back-breaking climb from the tube or bus stop with the shopping. That is one of the main aims of this book – to offer a wide choice of recipes from thoughtful and considerate chefs and restaurateurs to you, the attentive host and hostess, and to ensure that your dinners are a success whatever the occasion.

There is one other vital factor that made 'Lunch for a Fiver' a possibility and makes this recipe book a valuable addition to any bookshelf possibly already groaning with cook books.

Even five years ago it would have been impossible to launch 'Lunch for a Fiver' let alone make it a success because what we chose to eat would not. have allowed it. Then our choices still reflected this country's relatively recent conversion to *haute cuisine* and we were prepared to pay the prices that expensive raw ingredients – truffles, foie gras, large cuts of meat and fish – command even before they are cooked and served on expensive china.

Then came a massive sea-change, so big that it is impossible to pinpoint exactly when it started or where it came from. Certainly the hearty 'peasant' cooking of the southern Mediterranean took over from the more refined, more established food of France. California cooking became important, stressing the importance of good quality salads and vegetables, and cooks looked for inspiration even further east to Japan, Thailand and China. Olive oil replaced cream as grilling, now raised to an art form, replaced roasting. Health, personified in a well-balanced meal, became a priority.

For chefs who were aware of changing trends, who cared for their customers and who wanted to stay in business during the recession, this change in priorities came at a most opportune time. Dishes could be stripped of their most expensive single ingredient – meat, fish or poultry – and reworked so that two or three less expensive ingredients – sun-dried tomatoes, pasta and small strips of corn-fed chicken – shared the plate. It looked good and tasted good. And there was one other major advantage for chef and customer alike – it cost less.

This change in what and how we chose to eat can best be exemplified by the following comparison. When I was a restaurateur in the 1980s, with on average 450 customers a day to be looked after, our biggest supplier was the wholesale butcher. His monthly bill was around £10,000 and whenever the monthly gross food margin was not achieved this was the area we always looked at first to make savings. Today, for any busy chef or restaurateur, the priority is to find a first-class fruit and vegetable wholesaler who can reliably deliver, sometimes two or three times a day, the raw ingredients for the soups, salads that can be first courses or a significant proportion of the main courses, and the fruit that will at least tempt diners to break their promise and order a dessert.

In my article which launched 'Lunch for a Fiver', I wrote that it would be naive for any prospective diner to expect to be offered the most expensive raw ingredients – fillet steak, sea bass or wild mushrooms – for £5. But pasta, polenta, interesting and well-prepared vegetables, cheaper cuts of meat and less well known varieties of fish provide, in the hands of an imaginative chef, the basis for exciting food.

It is very obvious from the success of 'Lunch for a Fiver' that this approach is what we want today and that the chefs who took part in the scheme can deliver it successfully. The purpose of this book is to enable you to deliver the same enjoyable, healthy and inexpensive meals to your friends and family at home.

The origins of 'Lunch for a Fiver'

'Lunch for a Fiver' started with a newspaper cutting. Every six or eight weeks an old friend, Alex Bespaloff, New York's funniest wine writer, sits down and sends to Jancis and myself a small package of newspaper cuttings on food, restaurants and wine he has clipped from American magazines and newspapers, primarily the *New York Times*.

American journals do tend to give far more space to these subjects than English ones (a recent article Alex sent me calculated that a frequent restaurant-goer can spend £1700 a year on bottled water and cappucinos alone!) and one article from the *New York Times* was devoted to a promotional scheme devised by 100 top New York restaurateurs for the summer of 1992 offering a three-course lunch for US$19.92. The scheme was a huge success and the article included favourable comments not just from diners but also from many restaurateurs who had been overwhelmed by the response and planned to continue the scheme into the autumn.

Because the *Financial Times* is an international newspaper, my brief as restaurant reviewer is correspondingly wide. In my column in early September 1992 I wrote about the entrepreneurial imagination being shown by New York restaurateurs in the midst of the recession and wondered whether British restaurateurs would respond in a similar vein.

None did. The only man who read my article as enthusiastically as I had written it was my editor, Max Wilkinson. A Yorkshireman and a firm believer in value for money, he was growing increasingly exasperated at the prices he was being asked to pay for his business lunches, particularly in the City, and he rang me wondering whether we could organise something similar to the New York success.

I was excited at the prospect, subdued by the reality. The New York scheme seemed so original not only because it so cleverly tied the price of the meal to the calendar but also because it seemed a fair price for both sides. The restaurants were obviously discounting but at a price which at the then prevailing exchange rates (US$19.92 once equated to £10, remember?) and the customers were obviously getting a good deal.

In sterling nothing like this was possible. Trying to fit anything into 1993 in pounds and pence was impossible and lunches at £10 seemed to offer the customer no deal at all. There were already plenty of restaurants offering lunch at £9.95 and yet failing to fill their tables. £7.50 had no marketing ring to it at all. Desperate times, such as the onset of an economically bleak winter of 1992/3, called for desperate measures.

Max Wilkinson, Jane Scott, the *FT's* marketing manager, and I sat around the round table in Max's office (which just to set the tone economically looks across to a massive, entirely unlet, office block) and realised that only something for £5, an old-fashioned, much abused but still much-loved fiver, would do. It had the right ring to it and it would offer something that most people thought had long since disappeared. Where could you eat well for £5 when a take-away hamburger and chips cost £3?

I could not supply an answer. I agreed to go off and phone some of the chefs I knew well to gauge their reaction but I could not promise anything. We planned this scheme for late January, invari-ably the quietest trading period for any restaurant, but many I feared, might still find a 'fiver too little to swallow. In the Tube on the way home I kept asking myself the same question. If I was still the owner of L'Escargot, as I had been from 1980 to 1988, and some-one came to me with the outline of 'Lunch for a Fiver', what would my reaction have been?

At the end of the nine-stop Tube ride I had convinced myself that my answer would definitely have been positive. The reason was not so much the price which, even as an ex-restaurateur I realised was close to the bone, but the timing. As I sat on the Tube I recalled a scene that had taken place every year in my restaurant.

In any popular restaurant December is inordinately busy and hec-tic with Christmas and then New Year parties. Even business in early January can be good, catering for those sensitive enough to hold their celebrations after rather than before Christmas. But from the middle of January onwards the bookings book looks blank and February, with your customers paying off their credit bills from Christmas and the weather possibly very inhospitable, can be worse. An upturn comes with March, the longer evenings and finally a return to normal business after Easter.

This period also coincides with the worst period in any restau-rant's cash-flow. Trading pre-Christmas has been great, but closing on the bank holidays means no revenue: you have taken on extra staff to cope with all the parties but now the tables are empty. And all the suppliers' bills – from the usual sources but also including those for extra chairs, cutlery and crockery that have been hired specially – come rolling in.

What to do? My annual response was always the same and materialised in the scene that now came back to me so vividly on the Tube ride from Bank. About January 10 every year I would call a special management lunch about 2.30 pm (to work in the restaurant trade you have to be able to eat lunch and dinner at very unsociable hours) and with Elena Salvoni, the restaurant manager, Stephen Chamberlain, the brasserie manager and Martin Lam, the head chef, I would try to sound as pessimistic as I could about the forthcoming three months' trading. We must watch our overheads, cut our spending, allow anyone, however good, to leave if they wanted to and generally be extremely careful.

Such exhortations did work but the extraordinary thing in retrospect is that none of us tried to look at the other side of the equation. The restaurant business was extremely good in the mid to late 1980s so there was no long-term incentive to boost trade. We tried to cut costs and overheads but we never sat down and thought of original and exciting ways of bringing customers in. I did not think of 'Lunch for a Fiver' then when it would definitely have made some material difference to my company's management accounts. But now that it had lodged as an idea in my brain (and I am a very stubborn Mancunian) I quickly realised that I not only had all the reasons why 'Lunch for a Fiver' should work, but most of the answers to the objections that were bound to come from some very sceptical restaurateurs.

Once I had verbal support from two restaurateurs I went out and wrote to over 200 as we had all agreed that the scheme would only be successful if at least 100 restaurants took part. The response was terrible. Only a handful bothered to reply and they included the negative, thinly tinged with rudeness.

This response bore out an acute observation my wife made when she came into what passed for my office on the fourth floor of L'Escargot. Among the usual cacophony of phones ringing, intercom screeching and the photocopier churning out the daily specials, she wisely muttered 'in the restaurant trade there is no such thing as an in tray'.

And, after nine years in the business I have to agree with her. In the morning you are getting ready for the lunch service, trying to fit in dealing with the post, banking and other office duties. Then it is the service and at 2.30 pm time for your lunch. Late afternoon may be the time for some phone calls but the evening service can be busier than lunch and this may start as early as 5.30 pm if, as I was, you are in the West End with customers wanting to eat pre-theatre.

You then deal with the most immediate matters and put everything else in a pile to be dealt with as and when you need it. This is exactly what happened to my initial letter. I tried to make the package as enticing as possible. A two-page letter, an acceptance form and a copy of the Weekend *FT* constituted, I thought, an irresistible offer. All very professional but all to do with something that went into 'the pile' on the desks of restaurateurs up and down the country (if not the bin next to their desks) because it was not only potentially costly but it was not of the moment.

I then phoned all those who had not replied negatively and heard many objections, excuses and reasons for prevarication. But as the number of those who were prepared to back 'Lunch for a Fiver' increased, my confidence increased too. Many restaurateurs were obviously interested in the scheme if the price could be increased but I was determined not to change it. Another restaurateur argued that actually January was quite busy for him and it was February that was quiet. Could it be postponed a fortnight, he asked? I said no and argued that if January proved to be particularly busy thanks to 'Lunch for a Fiver' I was sure that it would spill over and February would be good too. Fortunately, I was proved right.

But the ten weeks I spent persuading restaurateurs to sign and send back their acceptance forms had one very important consequence for this book. When I sat down and wrote to all the chefs requesting their three-course menus, I made a point of asking for them a full month before they would be needed. Even so, very few arrived. I then sent out a reminder and they did start coming in. But the theory of the 'in tray' was proved valid, once again. The final recipe for this book arrived six weeks late!

The recipes and how to learn from professional chefs

When I bought L'Escargot in 1980 I was a lousy cook with no interest in becoming any better. My policy then was to hire the best chefs I could (including two featured in the book, Alastair Little and

Martin Lam of Ransome's Dock). Nine years later I had struggled to reach a reasonable standard and was determined to become even better. Today, I do all the cooking in our house.

There are two reasons for this change of heart. The first, I discovered quite quickly, is that during a restaurant's service there are only two places to be – looking after the customers or in the kitchen. The office is deadly quiet and I could not sit idly by taking up a table that could be occupied by a paying customer. As I am an appalling waiter, I started working in the kitchen, initially watching, then helping (often, I would be the first to admit, getting in the way) and finally doing the 'pass' – calling the orders – for the brasserie section.

I learnt because there were some very willing teachers – a phenomenon which has managed to make this book possible. Although certain chefs may be notorious for their ill humour, the majority are invariably kind, anxious to correct mistakes when they see others going wrong and willing, as many of these recipes prove, to pass on what in other industries would be considered 'trade secrets'.

It was not easy to prise these recipes out of the chefs but this was not because of their lack of generosity. Rather the opposite. They were all willing to sit down and spread the good word but many found it difficult to convert the dishes that they prepare instinctively, sometimes twice a day, into good written English. As I chivvied the chefs of Great Britain, back would come the following reply: 'One thing writing down these menus has done is to increase my respect for Elizabeth David, Jane Grigson, Delia Smith and Josceline Dimbleby. Their attention to detail, I now realise, must be absolutely fantastic.'

And in chasing round trying to compile all these recipes to meet the deadline I lost track of one important fact. Just how interesting they are, how varied, both in terms of raw ingredients and the time and skills necessary to prepare them properly, and just how much care and thought the chefs have put into supplying recipes that convert inexpensive ingredients into healthy food for the body and mind.

There are no favourites here, but many dishes that I have enjoyed. Jerusalem artichoke soup; mussel soup; cream of pea and lettuce soup; onion soup; banana curry soup; chick pea and bacon soup; spinach soup and London Particular, all good on a cold winter's day and easily convertible to cater for larger groups of friends.

And in line with the changing fashion on restaurant menus

where, to cater for those who are trying to eat less, particularly less red meat, the first courses are becoming more distinctive and more complicated, there are a number of recipes that will require additional time and patience. Quail's eggs on brioche with smoked salmon and spinach; Peppers Piedmontese; baked, stuffed jumbo mushrooms with balsamic vinegar; a warm salad of chicken livers; smoked haddock and gruyère tart; marinated salmon and mackerel; and, finally, a purée of smoked haddock.

Restaurant-goers' passion for salads and the cooking of the southern Mediterranean and Britain have been acknowledged. A warm lentil salad; a vinaigrette of broccoli, avocado and anchovies with shaved parmesan and a waterfall salad. Then on to spicy Italian sausages with a potato salad, perhaps, or a casserole of pheasant, duck and Toulouse sausages; lamb shanks with mashed potato; or individual pumpkin, oyster mushroom and ricotta filo parcels. From closer to home come the recipes for salmon Wellington and kedgeree; fish stew with leeks and saffron; venison casserole; pork chops with port and mushrooms; and Lancashire hotpot.

To look after two particular but different appetites there are recipes for spicy Thai dishes, a cheap but complicated Chinese meal and some delicious Indian dishes.

There are also quite enough recipes to keep those with a sweet tooth happy, including excitingly varied ways with cheap, healthy fruit – apples, pears, bananas and strawberries – plus a number that will impress with their sophistication such as hazelnut and white chocolate torte; frozen orange and ginger parfait; an iced mascarpone cream; and two different pavlovas.

Finally, to what many will consider the crux of this book – the cost of the menus. I would be the first to admit that despite the similar titles there are inherent contradictions between 'Lunch for a Fiver' and 'Dinner for a Fiver'. The former was a scheme to fill empty restaurant tables which it did successfully by offering a two-course lunch for £5 which, if it did not generate any profits, certainly had to cover the cost of the raw materials and go some way to contributing to the restaurant's running costs – wages, heat and light, laundry, rent and rates, etc.

None of these factors apply when you are cooking at home. You do not have to induce your friends, or family, to come round for what is for them effectively a free meal. Nor will you be remunerated for looking after your nearest and dearest, however much hard work you put into the meal.

But what we all need now is guidance on how to cook interesting, inexpensive meals that are certain to please because they are being served at some of the most popular restaurants up and down the country often twice a day. Some of these menus may involve more expensive ingredients than others but I do hope that the layout will encourage amateur chefs to plunder and adapt the professional chefs' recipes that are on offer to suit their friends and their budgets. Whenever I cook I invariably have a budget in mind, but it tends to become a 'moveable feast'. Cooking has become too enjoyable, my friends and family too important.

WINE FOR A FIVER

by Jancis Robinson

There has never, in the history of the wine-producing universe, been a better time to buy wine, and the most striking development over the last decade has been the improvement in the quality of wines retailing in Britain at less than £5 a bottle.

In sharp contrast to the 1960s and 1970s, nowadays you really have to work quite hard to find a wine that tastes nasty. Lack of distinction is the most common wine fault of the 1990s, which is probably regarded an offence only by people like me who spend their working lives analysing wines and wine styles.

The right wine to serve

Another way in which it seems to me we are particularly fortunate at the moment is that we live in such a libertarian era in terms of the foods and drinks we serve. At some point in the 1980s, 1970s for the really advanced, we seemed to agree to throw all previous rules and constraints into the rubbish bin and to eat and entertain in a much less rigidly structured way. A simple bowl of spaghetti and a glass of wine perhaps symbolises the new minimum input for what constitutes a meal: the spaghetti representing at least some form of culinary effort, the wine turning the meal into a social occasion.

A new generation of epicures has streamlined the entertaining process, discovering that there is a host of wines which can be drunk quite happily without food at the beginning of a meal, and with a wide range of foods throughout one. Practically any dry white, pink or red can perform this feat, so long as no one is expected to drink it with a pudding. (A sure sign that someone is drinking your wine without thinking is when they punctuate mouthfuls of the sweet course with a dry wine. A wine that is not at least as sweet as sweet food served with it really does taste disgusting.)

Red wine with meat and white wine with fish is an absurd and outdated generalisation. Matching the 'weight' of the wine (its alcohol level, or how unlike water it tastes, is a good guide) to the strength of flavours in a dish, or its heartiness, is much more important than the colour of the wine. And it is worth remembering that most peo-ple cannot tell red from white if they are blindfold, and if the wines are similar weights and served at the same temperature.

The art of finding the perfect wine to complement a particular dish is a complex one and would need an encyclopedic book of its own, in the unlikely event that anyone would want to buy it. Anyone interested enough in flavours and the sense of taste to be buying this book should have enough palate instinct to be able to trust to their own senses in putting a bottle and a dish together. But an open mind is just as important as a sensitive palate. A seriously sweet Riesling with creamy onion tart (leek and onion tart from Le Marché Noir, Edinburgh, page 89) was a runaway success the other night, probably because of the sweetness of onions themselves, and the sharp kick of acidity in the Riesling (try an example from Wash-ington State). Traditional wine lore has it that wine should not be served with anything acidic, such as salads and dishes such as Alis-tair Little's soused mackerel. Traditional wine lore probably never tried it. Many a vigorous young red wine is flattered by a bit of vine-gar or lemon juice, which can make the wine taste much softer and fuller in contrast. The tannins in young red wine, the preservatives that have the same effect on the mouth lining as cold tea, are said to pose problems for food matching. There is no doubt that a hunk of chewy meat softens those tannins, but who would have believed that taramasalata does the trick too? The smoked haddock on page 103 might well perform the same feat.

The most economical drink to serve with the delicious food on these pages is tap water, of course. Do what you will, but compare the effect on your palate of a mouthful of water and a mouthful of wine after tasting good, fresh garlic (as on page 40)

Be adventurous!

Where to buy

In the under £5 a bottle range, even I, a committed supporter of the independent specialist wine merchant, have to admit that the best bargains are to be found on the shelves of the supermarkets and off-licence chains. You will forfeit such valuable extras as advice, quan-tity discounts, glass loan, sale or return arrangements and delivery, however.

In general, most wine retailers are buying their wines from very similar sources; the only difference is in their selecting skills and buying muscle. The market has never been more cut-throat and competitive, and these are the major players (although their widest range will be stocked only at the biggest branches of the supermarkets and, in the case of the off-licence chains, only at designated Wine Shops):

Sainsbury's Very good prices, although occasionally dogged by the caution of a market leader.

Tesco A little more adventurous. They try harder.

Waitrose Excellent all-round wine supplier, although nothing too bargain basement.

Safeway Perhaps the most original and instinctive wine selection.

Thresher/Bottoms Up/Wine Rack Owned by brewers Whitbread. Not the cheapest, but run with real enthusiasm by and for wine lovers.

Victoria Wine/Augustus Barnett Good special offers. More workmanlike than rivals Thresher with a more restricted range.

Oddbins The quirkiest wine retailer is distinguished by its extras, especially the knowledge and enthusiasm of its staff. Oddbins has the flexibility to react quickly to the market.

Some particularly good buys

The wines included here are not necessarily the cheapest, but those that represent better value than most at under £5 a bottle.

● Eastern European wines in general, because their producers so desperately need hard currency and, an important bonus, their own winemakers are not too proud to take outside advice. Hungary has been a particularly useful source of good wines under £3, although there are had some good Slovakians of both colours. Romania has stocks of mature red at silly prices.

● The Languedoc in southern France, which supplies all those Vins de Pays d'Oc (its people being distinguished at one time by the way they said yes: *oc*). This vast area of southern France is dramatically revitalising itself, and only those who can offer sound wine-making and yields low enough to give properly ripe grapes will survive. A wide range of grape varieties is grown here (Tesco have been good at supplying many of them as single varietal wines), in a relatively consistent climate. Winemaking has improved, often as a result of Australian expertise. Also first rate value are Minervois and Corbières reds from ambitious domaines, which tend to cost just under £5 a bottle.

• Australian white wines, especially Rhine Riesling which really warrants a much higher price but has been desperately unfashionable, and is available in good supply. There are also some good value blended reds under a fiver (notably from Penfolds) – and few sparkling wines less than £5 taste as good as the Australian versions.

• Portuguese reds, and a few whites, carrying a brand name rather than one of the traditional appellations. These will have been specially designed for British palates and should therefore taste suitably juicy, but of refreshingly unfamiliar grape varieties, Portugal being one of the last countries to be invaded by the ubiquitous Cabernet Sauvignon and Chardonnay.

• Some Italian co-operatives are at last waking up to the requirements of the world wine market and making fruity, well priced whites and reds. Montepulciano d'Abruzzo still delivers more punch per penny than most red wines, but any inexpensive Italian with an unfamiliar name is worth trying.

• Fine, seriously old sherry has been available in absurdly underpriced half bottles at under a fiver, simply because sherry is unfashionable. There are few drinks better at sharpening the palate than a dry sherry, and some retailers such as Waitrose have been selling full bottles of richly mature sweet sherry for less than £5 which are divine with British and other hard cheeses.

• Watch out for Argentina, which can produce extremely juicy, full blooded reds, and aromatic dryish whites. Tesco's 'International Winemaker', Jacques Lurton, has led the way, but other cosmopolitan winemakers have followed him to the world's most seriously under-exploited vine resource.

• Sauvignon enthusiasts should look out for Jacques Lurton's Rueda whites from northern Spain, for Blayais Blanc from a livelier Bordeaux co-operative than most, and for Montana's basic New Zealand blend.

• And there should be no shortage of French wine bargains as producers in the Old World have to reduce prices to keep up with the New.

Part Two
THE RECIPES

ADLARD'S RESTAURANT
Norwich

Quails' Eggs on Brioche with Smoked Salmon and
Spinach

Puff Pillow of Mussels

Apple Charlotte with Crème Anglaise

Serves 4

Quails' Eggs on Brioche with Smoked Salmon and Spinach

12 quails' eggs
225 g (8 oz) spinach,
  washed
4 slices of brioche, 1 cm
  (½ inch) thick
butter

salt and pepper
grated nutmeg
300 ml (½ pint) white wine
  sauce
50 g (2 oz) smoked salmon,
  diced

1. Plunge the quails' eggs into rapidly boiling water. Cook for exactly 2 minutes, then plunge into iced water.
2. When cold, peel the eggs carefully (if you leave them in the refrigerator in water overnight, they are easier to peel). They should be soft. (These eggs are delicate; you will probably need 'spares'.) Put the eggs in cold water and store in the refrigerator.
3. Blanch the spinach and refresh in cold water. Squeeze out as much water as possible.
4. Toast the brioche on both sides. Cut out a circle 5 cm (2 inches) across with a round cutter. Keep warm.
5. Sauté the spinach in butter and season with salt, pepper and nutmeg.
6. Plunge the quails' eggs in very hot water for 30 seconds. Drain and season. Boil up the sauce and add the smoked salmon.
7. Put the spinach on top of the brioche and 'nestle' the quails' eggs into the spinach. Gently pour the sauce with smoked salmon on top of the quails' eggs.

Puff Pillow of Mussels

48–60 mussels
about 225 g (8 oz) puff
  pastry
beaten egg, to glaze
clarified butter, to glaze

*Curry White Wine Shallot
Sauce:*
2 large shallots, skinned and
  finely diced

200 ml (7 fl oz) dry white
  wine
7.5 ml (1½ tsp) curry
  powder
50 ml (2 fl oz) white wine
  vinegar
15 ml (1 tbsp) double cream
225 g (8 oz) unsalted butter
salt and pepper

1. Clean the mussels, discarding beards and limpets. Put them in a
   pan with a little water, cover and cook over a high heat. Do not
   cook them too much, they will go leathery. When the shells are
   open, transfer them to a tray. Take out the mussels, and check if
   the beards are still there. If so, pick them off. Throw away the
   mussels which are not open.
2. For the sauce, reduce the shallots, wine, curry powder and vinegar until dry. Add the cream and bring to the boil. Over a low
   heat, add a small amount of butter at a time, whisking it in. Careful with the temperature, when the mixture is too cold or too hot
   the sauce will separate. Season to taste. The consistency should
   be 'creamy'. Keep warm.
3. Roll out the puff pastry, cut into 4 rectangles 9 × 10 cm × 3 mm
   (3½ × 4 × ⅛ inch). Rest in the refrigerator or freezer.
4. Brush the top with egg glaze and place on a baking sheet. Bake
   in the oven at 190°C (375°F) mark 5 until golden brown. Split
   the puff pastry squares horizontally and spoon out the uncooked
   pastry from the middle. Before serving, warm in the oven.
5. Put the base of the warmed puff pastry base in the middle of the
   plate. Pile the mussels (12–15 per person) in the middle and
   pour on the sauce. Top the mussels with the puff pastry 'pillow'
   glazed with clarified butter.

Apple Charlotte with Crème Anglaise

450 g (1 lb) Bramley apples
butter for sautéeing
sugar
cinnamon or nutmeg
lemon juice
white bread, preferably
 brioche (the bread must
 be firm)
clarified butter for soaking
 bread

Crème Anglaise:
300 ml (½ pint) double
 cream
300 ml (½ pint) milk
½ vanilla pod
75 g (3 oz) sugar
6 egg yolks

1. Peel, core and cut apples in 1 cm (½ inch) cubes. Sauté the apple cubes quickly in butter so the apples do not brown. Add sugar to taste, cinnamon or nutmeg and lemon juice to taste. Leave the apples undercooked. (They will cook more when you cook the charlotte.)
2. Line the base of a pudding mould with greaseproof paper. Cut the bread 3 mm (⅛ inch) thick. Soak in clarified butter and use to line the mould. Press the apple in firmly, pressing down hard. Cover the apple with bread and then cover the pudding mould with foil.
3. Cook in the oven at 230°C (450°F) mark 8 for 20 minutes. After 15 minutes, examine the side of the charlotte to see if the bread is brown.
4. Meanwhile for the Crème Anglaise, infuse the cream and milk with the vanilla pod in a pan. Bring almost to the boil.
5. Whisk the sugar and egg yolks together in a bowl. Pour on the milk and cream and mix. Pour back into the saucepan and heat, stirring, until thickened. Pass through a sieve.
6. Unmould the charlotte onto a plate which has a pool of Crème Anglaise on the base.

ALASTAIR LITTLE
London W1

Soused Mackerel
Spicy Sausages with Potato Salad
Pain Perdu from Burnley

Serves 4–6

Soused Mackerel

1 carrot, peeled
1 inside stick from a celery
   head with leaves
1 red onion, skinned
150 ml (¼ pint) dry white
   wine
150 ml (¼ pint) good quality
   white wine vinegar

1 bay leaf
6 peppercorns
15 ml (1 tbsp) Maldon salt
15 ml (1 tbsp) caster sugar
two 225 g (8 oz) mackerel,
   cleaned and filleted

1. Slice the carrot and celery 3 mm (⅛ inch) thick. Slice the onion into 3 mm (⅛ inch) half rounds.
2. Combine the wine, vinegar, carrot, celery, onion, bay leaf, peppercorns, salt and sugar in a saucepan. Bring to the boil and simmer for 15 minutes.
3. With a slotted spoon remove half the vegetables from the 'souse' and place them in the base of a roasting dish.
4. Arrange the mackerel fillets, skin side up, on this bed and strew with the remaining vegetables.
5. Return the sousing liquid to the boil and pour over mackerel. Cover with greaseproof paper, cut to fit the inside of the dish. Cook in the oven at 180°C (350°F) mark 4 for about 20 minutes. Remove and allow to cool before serving.

Spicy Sausages with Potato Salad

900 g (2 lb) large new
  potatoes, scrubbed
15 ml (1 tbsp) Dijon
  mustard
15 ml (1 tbsp) red wine
  vinegar
30 ml (2 tbsp) skinned and
  thinly sliced shallots

30 ml (2 tbsp) flat parsley
  leaves
salt and pepper
60 ml (4 tbsp) extra virgin
  olive oil
sunflower oil for cooking
700–900 g (1½–2 lb) spicy
  Italian sausages

1. Cook and slice the potatoes, then return to the saucepan. They should be slightly undercooked.
2. To make the dressing, combine the mustard, vinegar, shallots and parsley in a salad bowl. Season. Beat in the olive oil and set aside.
3. Lightly oil a frying pan and arrange the sausages in it. Add water to half cover the sausages and put the pan over a medium heat. Cook until the water has evaporated and the sausages are starting to sizzle. Turn them at this point. Continue cooking, turning occasionally and basting until they are relatively evenly browned and cooked, about 30 minutes.
4. As the sausages near completion, pour some of the liquid over the potato slices to cover and quickly heat through. Do not boil or the potato slices will disintegrate. Drain and toss in the bowl with the dressing.
5. To serve, place two or more sausages per person on a bed of warm potato salad.

Pain Perdu from Burnley

**4 thick slices of ordinary
white bread, crusts
removed
50 g (2 oz) unsalted butter
60 ml (4 tbsp) good quality
strawberry or raspberry
jam**

Batter:
**100 ml (4 fl oz) double
cream
3 egg yolks
45 ml (3 tbsp) caster sugar
icing sugar for dusting**

1. For the batter, combine the cream, egg yolks and caster sugar in a bowl and stir until evenly mixed. Transfer to a flat bottomed dish.
2. To assemble the sandwiches, butter the bread lightly and cut diagonally. Spread one triangle with jam and sandwich with the other. You now have 4 triangular 'butties'.
3. Heat the remaining butter over a low to medium heat in a frying pan. Meanwhile, dip the sandwiches in the batter, press lightly, turn and remove carefully. Place them into the hot butter (take care the butter does not burn).
4. Cook for 3–4 minutes. Turn gingerly and cook for 3–4 minutes on the other side until golden brown. Remove from the pan and drain on absorbent kitchen paper. Dust with icing sugar and serve.

THE ARGYLL
London SW3

Jerusalem Artichoke and Salsify Soup
Calves' Liver with Fried Sage and Purée of Potatoes
Millefeuille of Strawberries

Serves 4

Jerusalem Artichoke and Salsify Soup

1.1 litres (2 pints) water
500 ml (17 fl oz) olive oil
1 sprig of thyme
1 clove of garlic, skinned
25 g (1 oz) coriander seeds
200 ml (7 fl oz) white wine
  vinegar
1 lemon, sliced
salt
5 Jerusalem artichokes
10 sticks of salsify
100 ml (4 fl oz) double
  cream
sprig of coriander, to garnish

1. Take all the ingredients, except the artichokes, salsify and cream, and boil together for 5 minutes.
2. Scrub and peel the artichokes and salsify and add whole to the stock. Simmer for 30 minutes until the artichokes are soft. Leave to cool, then purée in a blender.
3. Reheat the soup, add the cream and check the seasoning. Serve with a sprig of coriander to garnish.

Note: Sliced shi-itake mushrooms are excellent served with this soup.

Calves' Liver with Fried Sage and Purée of Potatoes

450 g (1 lb) calves' liver, cut
   in 4 thin slices
flour for dusting
1 egg yolk
50 g (2 oz) breadcrumbs
700 g (1½ lb) King Edward
   potatoes, peeled
salt and pepper

50 ml (2 fl oz) milk
1 shallot, skinned and sliced
1 sprig of thyme
1 clove of garlic, skinned
50 ml (2 fl oz) double cream
50 g (2 oz) butter
oil and butter for frying
2 sprigs of sage leaves

1. Dust the slices of calves' liver with flour. Brush with egg yolk,
   then coat with breadcrumbs.
2. Boil the potatoes in salted water. Drain and finely mash.
3. Boil the milk and add shallot, thyme and garlic for 2 minutes.
   Strain and add to the potatoes. Blend in the cream and butter to
   form quite a runny purée. Check the seasoning
4. Pan fry the calves' liver until golden brown. Fry the sage leaves.
5. To serve, pour potato purée onto 4 warm plates, place the liver
   on top and garnish with sage leaves.

Millefeuille of Strawberries

6 sheets of filo pastry
50 g (2 oz) melted butter
200 g (7 fl oz) whipped
   cream

20 ml (¾ oz) icing sugar
10 good large strawberries,
   sliced

1. Brush all the sheets of filo with melted butter. Layer 3 sheets
   together twice bound by the butter to form 2 layered sheets.
2. Cut out 12 rounds using a round 10 cm (4 inch) cutter (6 from
   each sheet). Bake in the oven at 200°C (400°F) mark 6 for about
   2–3 minutes or until golden brown. Cool.
3. Pipe cream onto 8 of the rounds and dust the remaining 4 with
   icing sugar.
4. Place sliced strawberries on top of the cream and build up 4
   millefeuille with the dusted rounds on top.

AU JARDIN DES GOURMETS
London, W1

Mussel Soup
Braised Knuckle of Veal with Lemon
Orange Cake

Serves 4

Mussel Soup

2 litres (4 pints) mussels
1 carrot, peeled and finely chopped
2 shallots, skinned and finely chopped
25 g (1 oz) butter
450 ml (¾ pint) dry white wine

sprig of parsley, finely chopped
450 ml (¾ pint) water
salt and pepper
45 ml (3 tbsp) double cream

1. Scrub the mussels and scrape off their beards, discarding any mussels that do not shut tightly. Place in a large saucepan, cover and cook for about 10 minutes until the shells open. Remove from the heat as soon as they are open.
2. In another saucepan, gently fry the carrot and shallots in butter, without browning. When the shallots are tender, add the white wine and continue cooking.
3. Strain the mussels and add their liquor to the soup. Shell the mussels and add to the soup with the parsley. Pour in the 450 ml (¾ pint) water and bring to the boil. Season to taste. Just before serving, take the pan off the heat and add the cream.

Braised Knuckle of Veal with Lemon

50 g (2 oz) butter
4 pieces shin of veal cut across the bone, about 225–275 g (8–10 oz) each
2 onions, skinned and chopped
5 carrots, peeled and sliced
1 stick of celery, chopped

5 tomatoes, skinned
salt and pepper
2 bay leaves
grated zest of 1 lemon
250 ml (8 fl oz) dry white wine
juice of 3 lemons

1. Melt the butter in a flameproof casserole. Add the meat, onions, carrots and celery and cook until veal is brown.
2. Add the tomatoes, salt, pepper, bay leaves and the lemon zest. Moisten with the white wine and 250 ml (8 fl oz) water. Cover and cook for 1–1½ hours.
3. Remove the meat and vegetables from the casserole with a slotted spoon or skimmer. Arrange in a dish and keep hot. Add the lemon juice to the cooking liquor. Bring to the boil and spoon this sauce over the meat. Serve with rice.

Orange Cake

400 g (14 oz) granulated sugar
2 round almond cake layers
300 g (11 oz) orange marmalade

60 ml (4 tbsp) Cointreau
100 g (4 oz) plain chocolate
25 g (1 oz) butter
1 orange, sliced

1. To make a sugar syrup, combine the sugar with 350 ml (12 fl oz) water in a pan. Bring to the boil and continue to boil over a high heat until the sugar totally dissolves. Remove from the heat and cool before using.
2. Split the cake layers horizontally. Melt the orange marmalade thoroughly in 100 ml (4 fl oz) water over a low heat and then stack the cake layers as follows: place one layer on a plate and pour over some of the marmalade mixture and 15 ml (1 tbsp) Cointreau. Place the second layer over the first and repeat.
3. Meanwhile, melt the chocolate and butter together, mixing thoroughly. Use this mixture to frost the cake. Glaze the orange slices in the sugar syrup and use to decorate the cake.

BAHN THAI
London, W1

Fried Spring Rolls
Plum Sauce
Minced Beef with Chillies and Holy Basil
Squid Fried with Yellow Beans

Serves 4

Fried Spring Rolls

1.00 g (4 oz) pack bean
  vermicelli
350 g (12 oz) carrot, peeled
350 g (12 oz) white cabbage
175 g (6 oz) onion, skinned
15 ml (1 tbsp) cooking oil
2 cloves of garlic, skinned
  and finely chopped

350 g (12 oz) minced pork
100 g (4 oz) bean sprouts
salt and white pepper
1 pack Small or Medium
  Spring Roll Wrappers,
  thawed
1 egg
oil for deep frying

1. Soak the vermicelli in cold water for 10 minutes. Cut the carrot, cabbage and onion into small julienne strips (matchstick size or smaller). When the vermicelli is soft, cut into 5 cm (2 inch) lengths with a sharp knife or kitchen scissors.
2. Heat the oil in a wok until it is smoking hot. Add the garlic, quickly followed by the minced pork. Stir fry until the pork is cooked, then add the onion, carrot, cabbage, vermicelli and bean sprouts. Stir fry until they are soft. Remove the wok from the heat, season to taste and set aside to cool.
3. Separate the spring roll wrappers (they are normally stuck together but peel back quite easily) and lay them out on a clean work surface. Beat the egg in a bowl and place it beside the wrappers.
4. When the filling is cool, place a spoonful near the corner of a wrapper sheet. (Use 10 ml (2 tsp) for small wrappers or 15 ml (1 tbsp) for medium sheets.) Then fold over the corner nearest

the filling to cover the filling. Fold over the 2 side corners to form an envelope and brush beaten egg on the remaining flap. Roll the filling towards the remaining flap to form a completed spring roll. Repeat the procedure with further sheets of wrapper until the filling is used up.

5. The spring rolls, in this form, keep for about 24 hours in the refrigerator or much longer in an airtight container in the freezer. When you wish to cook them, heat oil in a deep fryer to 170°C (325°F). Drop in the spring rolls gently and fry until golden brown. Serve with a small bowl of plum sauce for dipping.

Plum Sauce

2 red peppers
4–5 large red chillies
100 g (4 oz) preserved
  bottled plums

900 g (2 lb) granulated
  sugar
150 ml (¼ pint) distilled
  vinegar

1. Remove the stalks from the peppers and chillies and discard. Either chop very finely or put in a food processor until very finely minced.
2. Rub the plums through your fingers to break up the flesh, do not discard the stones.
3. Mix together the sugar and 600 ml (1 pint) water in a saucepan, put on a medium heat and bring to the boil. When the syrup is boiling well, add the minced peppers and chillies with the plums.
4. Bring back to the boil and allow to boil for 2–3 minutes, then add the vinegar. The resulting sauce should be sweet and sour. Allow the sauce to cool. Remove and discard the plum stones, then bottle the sauce.

Minced Beef with Chillies and Holy Basil

Select ordinary chillies or the tiny hot 'bird' chillies, depending on your taste for spiciness. With plain rice, this is one of Thailand's most popular midday snack meals.

6 chillies
2 cloves of garlic, skinned
oil for frying
175 g (6 oz) minced beef

18–20 Thai Holy basil leaves
  or ordinary basil
fish sauce

1. Hit the chillies with the side of a knife, then slice them into pieces lengthwise. Very finely chop or pound the garlic.
2. Heat the oil in a wok or frying pan and add the garlic. As the garlic starts to turn golden, add the meat and stir to break up the lumps. Keep stirring until the meat is half cooked, then add the chillies and continue to stir.
3. When the meat is fully cooked, add the basil leaves. Stir them in, then season to taste with fish sauce and serve.
4. If this dish is being eaten as a one dish meal, serve over a mound of steamed rice with a small bowl of fish sauce. Accompany with some thinly sliced chillies beside the plate to alter the seasoning. It tastes particularly good if eaten in the Thai manner with a fried egg on top.

Squid Fried with Yellow Beans

175 g (6 oz) squid, the
  smaller the better
15 ml (1 tbsp) oil
30 ml (2 tbsp) salted yellow
  beans
15 ml (1 tbsp) vinegar

30 ml (2 tbsp) fish or
  chicken stock
2 spring onions, trimmed
  and thinly sliced
fish sauce
pepper

1. Remove the skin and innards from the squid, then cut it into 2.5 cm (1 inch) squares. Lightly draw the blade of a knife across the squid, cutting a diamond pattern into the flesh but not through.
2. Heat the oil in a wok and add the yellow beans. Stir well, then add the squid, vinegar, stock and spring onions. Stir well until lightly cooked. Turn out onto a plate and season to taste with fish sauce and pepper. Serve.

BEAUCHAMP'S
London, EC3

Grilled Garlic Mussels
Salmon Wellington
Bank of England Pudding

Serves 4–6

Grilled Garlic Mussels

8–10 mussels per person, cleaned
600 ml (1 pint) white wine
100 g (4 oz) breadcrumbs
7 g (¼ oz) chopped fresh parsley

6 cloves of garlic, skinned and finely chopped
2 shallots, skinned and finely chopped
100 g (4 oz) melted butter
salt and pepper

1. Cook the mussels in half the white wine. When open, remove one shell from each mussel. Discard any mussels which do not open.
2. Turn the grill to a high heat and lay the mussels in a flameproof dish.
3. Place the breadcrumbs in a bowl with the rest of the ingredients and mix well. Sprinkle this mixture over the mussels and glaze under the grill until golden brown.

Salmon Wellington

1 kg (2¼ lb) salmon fillet
1 onion, skinned and
    chopped
butter for cooking
350 g (12 oz) cooked rice
600 ml (1 pint) béchamel
    sauce
3 hard-boiled eggs, roughly
    chopped
25 g (1 oz) fresh parsley,
    chopped
450 g (1 lb) puff pastry

175 g (6 oz) spinach,
    washed and cooked
beaten egg to glaze

Court bouillon:
splash of vinegar
20 peppercorns
salt
6 bay leaves
150 ml (¼ pint) white wine
parsley stalks

1. Put the ingredients for the court bouillon in a pan and heat. Poach the salmon in the court bouillon until half cooked, about 10 minutes. Leave to one side.
2. Gently fry the onion in a little butter. Add the cooked rice, 150 ml (¼ pint) of the béchamel sauce, the hard-boiled eggs and parsley. Cook this mixture slowly for 5 minutes.
3. Roll out the puff pastry into a rectangular shape, twice the size of the fillet of salmon. Along one side of the rectangle in the middle – where you are going to place the fish – spread out the spinach. Place the salmon on top and cover with the sauce.
4. Brush the puff pastry with beaten egg. Roll over the salmon, pinching the ends and rolling them in.
5. Brush the Wellington with beaten egg. Bake in the oven at 180°C (350°F) mark 4 for 40 minutes.
6. To serve, slice into thick portions and pour over the remaining béchamel sauce.

Bank of England Pudding

This pudding was served to the sergeant of the regiment who used to guard the Bank of England!

1.4 kg (3 lb) Bramley apples
175 g (6 oz) butter
225 g (8 oz) sugar
7.5 ml (1½ tsp) ground mixed spice

175 g (6 oz) plain flour
salt
100 g (4 oz) broken walnuts
50 g (2 oz) icing sugar
lemon juice to moisten

1. Peel and core the apples, then slice. Place 50 g (2 oz) of the butter in a pan with 100 g (4 oz) of the sugar, the mixed spice and sliced apples. Cook slowly until soft.
2. In a large bowl, place the flour, remaining butter and sugar and a pinch of salt. Rub together until a fine crumble is formed.
3. In an ovenproof dish, place the walnuts, icing sugar and a sprinkling of lemon juice. Glaze these in the oven at 180°C (350°F) mark 4 for 5 minutes. When the walnuts are cool, mix into the crumble.
4. Spread the apples in an ovenproof dish and cover with the walnut crumble topping. Bake in the oven for 40 minutes or until the top is golden and crisp. Serve with double cream, vanilla ice cream or crème fraîche.

BELGO
London, NW1

Green Soup
Mussels with Bacon in Beer
Sweet Waffles

Serves 4–6

Green Soup

100 g (4 oz) butter
75 g (3 oz) onion, skinned
75 g (3 oz) celery
75 g (3 oz) leek, washed
75 g (3 oz) peeled potato
1 clove of garlic, skinned
100 g (4 oz) plain flour
1.7 litres (3 pints) chicken
  stock
1 bay leaf

sprig of thyme
2 bunches of watercress,
  trimmed and washed
100 g (4 oz) spinach,
  trimmed and washed
2 bunches of chervil
salt and pepper
grated nutmeg
15 ml (1 tbsp) whipped
  cream and chives

1. Melt the butter in a pan and sweat the onion, celery, leek, potato and garlic until soft. Add the flour and cook for a few minutes.
2. Stir in the chicken stock, bay leaf and thyme, then simmer for 15 minutes. Add the watercress, spinach and chervil, then cook for 5 minutes.
3. Purée the soup in a blender or food processor, then sieve through a conical strainer.
4. Season with salt, pepper and nutmeg, and garnish with a whirl of whipped cream and chives. Serve hot or cold.

Note: In order to retain the vivid green colour of the soup, it is important to place the conical strainer over a container placed on ice, so that the soup cools as quickly as possible.

Mussels with Bacon in Beer

50 g (2 oz) smoked bacon
25 g (1 oz) onion
25 g (1 oz) celery
1 kg (2 lb) mussels
sprig of thyme

50 ml (2 fl oz) Leffe
    Radieuse or light beer
50 g (2 oz) butter
25 g (1 oz) plain flour
pepper

1. Cut the bacon into julienne strips and fry until golden brown. Add the onion and celery and cook for a further minute.
2. Add the mussels, thyme and beer, increase the heat and cover with a lid.
3. Mix the butter and flour to a paste. When the mussels are cooked, add the butter and flour mixture in pieces to thicken. Simmer for 20 seconds. Add pepper to taste and serve.

Sweet Waffles

250 g (9 oz) plain flour
75 ml (3 fl oz) warm milk
25 g (1 oz) fresh yeast
1 egg
1 egg yolk
pinch of salt

12 g (½ oz) sugar
dash of vanilla essence
pinch of ground cinnamon
175 g (6 oz) soft butter
160 g (5½ oz) pearl sugar

1. Mix to a dough all the ingredients, except the butter and pearl sugar. Rest the dough for 30 minutes, covered with a damp cloth.
2. Knead in the soft butter. Finally add the pearl sugar.
3. Divide the dough into 75 g (3 oz) portions and leave for 30 minutes before cooking.
4. Preheat a waffle iron. Place two portions onto each iron and cook for 3 minutes. Serve immediately.

LA BELLE EPOQUE
Belfast

Cream Soup of Fresh Peas and Lettuce
Salmon Ravioli
Strawberry Cream Pots

Serves 4

Cream Soup of Fresh Peas and Lettuce

75 g (3 oz) butter
700 g (1½ lb) fresh baby
  peas
3 small round lettuces, finely
  chopped
7.5 ml (½ tbsp) plain flour
1.4 litres (2½ pints) chicken
  stock

salt and white pepper
pinch of sugar
150 ml (¼ pint) whipped
  cream
sprig of chervil, to garnish

1. Melt the butter in a saucepan and cook the shelled peas and lettuce, without colouring, for 5 minutes.
2. Sprinkle in the flour and stir with a wooden spoon until smooth. Add the stock and seasonings and bring to the boil. Simmer for 20 minutes.
3. Purée the soup in a blender, then pass through a fine strainer. Adjust the consistency with chicken stock if the soup is too thick.
4. Check the seasoning, and serve with a whirl of whipped cream and chervil. This soup can be served hot or cold. (If you serve it chilled, add a little more salt.)

Salmon Ravioli

Pasta:
250 g (9 oz) plain flour
1.25 ml (¼ tsp) salt
1.25 ml (¼ tsp) olive oil
2 eggs
3 egg yolks

salt and pepper
grated nutmeg
cayenne pepper
300 ml (½ pint) double
    cream

Filling:
250 g (9 oz) salmon trout,
    skinned and boned

1. For the pasta, mix the flour, salt, olive oil, eggs and egg yolks into a dough.
2. Knead the pasta dough well until even and smooth. Wrap in clingfilm and allow to rest for 20 minutes in the refrigerator.
3. Preferably using a pasta machine, roll out the dough as finely as possible.
4. For the filling, mince the salmon trout finely. Season with salt, pepper, nutmeg and cayenne pepper.
5. Put the minced salmon trout in a blender and add the cream slowly. Pass the mixture through a fine sieve and keep cool. Adjust seasoning as necessary.
6. Put teaspoons of the salmon mousse on the pasta at 2.5 cm (1 inch) intervals and cover with another sheet of pasta. Cut into shapes with a ravioli wheel.
7. Cook the pasta in lots of boiling salted water until just cooked. Serve with a white wine sauce.

Strawberry Cream Pots

225 g (8 oz) fresh
  strawberries
300 ml (½ pint) double
  cream
45 ml (3 tbsp) caster sugar

20–30 ml (4–6 tsp) Curaçao
  or Cointreau
3–4 egg yolks, size 6
whipped cream and 4
  strawberries, to serve

1. Purée the strawberries in a blender. Add the cream, and stir in the sugar and liqueur. Blend in the strawberries.
2. Whisk the egg yolks until thick and creamy. Pour onto the strawberry cream, then whip the mixture lightly. Pour it through a sieve.
3. Put the mixture into 4 ramekins and place in a bain marie. Cover with foil. Cook in the oven at 150°C (300°F) mark 2 for about 30 minutes or until firm to touch.
4. Chill the desserts. To serve, pipe a rosette of cream on each and place a strawberry on top.

BOYD'S
London, W8

Chick Pea and Bacon Soup
Twice Cooked Leg of Duck with Red Cabbage
Bread and Butter Pudding with Whisky

Serves 4–6

Chick Pea and Bacon Soup

450 g (1 lb) chick peas
1 large onion, skinned and
  chopped
4 cloves of garlic, skinned
  and chopped
100 g (4 oz) smoked streaky
  bacon, chopped

butter and oil for cooking
chicken stock
bouquet garni
100 g (4 oz) smoked back
  bacon, cubed
pepper
cream, to finish

1. Soak the chick peas in water for 24 hours.
2. Sweat the onion, garlic and streaky bacon in butter and oil until translucent.
3. Drain and add the chick peas. Cover with chicken stock, add the bouquet garni and cook until the chick peas are very soft.
4. Grill the cubes of back bacon. Purée the soup in a blender, then pass through a sieve. Adjust seasoning.
5. Reheat the soup, add cream to taste and garnish with the cubes of back bacon.

Twice-Cooked Leg of Duck with Red Cabbage

Duck:
2 large carrots, peeled and
  chopped
4 sticks of celery, chopped
1 large onion, skinned and
  chopped
1 bulb of garlic, skinned
butter and oil for cooking
4–6 duck legs
1 bottle red wine
bouquet garni
honey

Red cabbage:
1 onion, skinned and sliced
4 cloves of garlic, skinned
  and sliced
butter and oil for cooking
1 small red cabbage, sliced
white wine vinegar
sugar
salt and pepper

1. Cook the vegetables in butter and oil in a casserole until soft. Add the duck legs, then half cover with red wine.
2. Add the bouquet garni. Bring to the boil, cover and cook in the oven at 200°C (400°F) mark 6 for 30–40 minutes or until the duck is cooked.
3. Meanwhile for the red cabbage, sweat the onion and garlic in butter and oil to soften. Add the red cabbage and toss.
4. Add white wine vinegar to taste. Cook uncovered until the vinegar is absorbed. Season with sugar, salt and pepper.
5. Transfer the duck to a metal plate. Paint with honey and replace in the oven for about 10 minutes or until golden brown and crispy. Serve on the red cabbage.
6. While the duck is cooking in the oven, reduce the cooking juices to demi glace, pass through a strainer and season. Use as the sauce. Serve the duck on top of the red cabbage.

Bread and Butter Pudding with Whisky

4 eggs
90 g (3½ oz) sugar
600 ml (1 pint) milk
1 vanilla pod, split
1 large measure whisky
  (or more)

bread or French stick, one
  day old
butter for spreading
sultanas

1. Mix the eggs and sugar together in a bowl. Boil the milk with the vanilla pod. Add the milk to the egg mixture, removing the vanilla. Add the whisky.
2. Cut the bread into slices about 1 cm (½ inch) thick. (Allow 3 slices per person.) Butter them. Arrange 3 slices in each of 4–6 large individual ramekins, then sprinkle over sultanas. Pour the custard equally over each ramekin.
3. Bake in a bain marie in the oven at 200°C (400°F) mark 6 for about 20 minutes.

THE BRACKENBURY
London, W6

Peppers Piedmontese
Grilled Grey Mullet with Roast Fennel
Pecan Pie

Serves 4–6

Peppers Piedmontese

8 plum tomatoes
4 red peppers, halved and
  seeded
4 cloves of garlic, skinned
  and finely chopped

salt and pepper
olive oil
marinated anchovy fillets

1. Blanch the tomatoes, refresh in cold water and skin. Halve the tomatoes and remove the pulp.
2. Lay the peppers in a roasting tray (open side up), put 5 ml (1 tsp) garlic inside each and 2 tomato halves. Season well.
3. Pour a little olive oil and water in the bottom of the tray and bake in the oven at 150°C (300°F) mark 2 for about 45 minutes. Take care not to burn the bottoms. The peppers are cooked when they feel tender when you pinch them.
4. Serve warm or cold with a few anchovy fillets placed on top. Be sure to pour a little of the cooking juices on to each serving.

Grilled Grey Mullet with Roast Fennel

4–6 large heads of fennel
4–6 red onions, skinned and
   halved
salt and pepper
sprigs of thyme
sprigs of rosemary
1.4 kg (3 lb) spinach,
   washed

butter for cooking
four to six 175 g (6 oz)
   fillets
   of grey mullet
lemon juice
lemon oil/(optional)

1. Halve the bulbs of fennel, removing the stalky bits. Lay the fennel and onions, flat surface down, on an oiled tray (garlic oil is best). Season and scatter some thyme and rosemary over the vegetables.
2. Place in the oven at 200°C (400°F) mark 6. Turn the vegetables over halfway through. Both onions and fennel should be golden brown on the flat surface. When ready, keep warm (not hot).
3. Cook the spinach in a heavy bottomed pan in butter and season. Sprinkle the skin side of the fish with sea salt and a little oil. Place under a hot grill.
4. Meanwhile put the spinach on plates with the roast vegetables. Flip the fish – the skin should be very crispy. The fish is ready when it is still slightly translucent in the middle. Just before removing from the grill, squeeze a little lemon juice on each fillet. Put on plates and drizzle over a little lemon oil.

Note: the grey mullet should be spanking fresh. Red mullet can also be used, but will cost you a lot more.

Pecan Pie

Sweet pastry:
225 g (8 oz) butter
450 g (1 lb) plain flour
60 g (2¼ oz) sugar
1 egg
90 ml (6 tbsp) milk

Filling:
225 g (8 oz) shelled pecans
250 g (8 oz) golden syrup
3 eggs
75 g (3 oz) butter, melted

1. For the pastry, cut the butter into small cubes. Mix the flour, sugar and butter together by rubbing the butter through your fingertips until the mixture looks like fine breadcrumbs. This can be done in a food processor. Add the egg and milk, little by little, until the pastry forms a ball.
2. Roll out and line a pastry case. Put in the refrigerator for about 10 minutes to chill. Bake blind in the oven at 190°C (375°F) mark 5 for 15 minutes.
3. For the filling, put the pecans in the pastry case. Whisk the syrup, eggs and melted butter together and pour onto the pecans. Bake for about 20–30 minutes until the filling is quite solid.

Today
Fishermans
pie

BRASSERIE DU MARCHE AUX PUCES
London, W10

Pan Fried Chicken Livers with Mixed Leaves
Pumpkin, Oyster Mushroom and Ricotta Filo Parcels
Hazelnut and White Chocolate Torte

Serves 6

Pan-fried Chicken Livers with Mixed Leaves

450 g (1 lb) mixed leaves, such as oakleaf, dandelion, mâche, frisée
150 ml (¼ pint) virgin olive oil
700 g (1½ lb) chicken livers, trimmed
salt and pepper
50 ml (2 fl oz) balsamic vinegar
juice of 1 lemon
chopped chives

1. Wash the salad leaves and divide between the plates.
2. Heat the olive oil in a pan and fry the chicken livers for 2–3 minutes with salt and pepper depending on how pink you like them.
3. Remove the chicken livers and pour off the sediment. Add balsamic vinegar, lemon juice, olive oil and chives.
4. Place the chicken livers over the salad leaves and pour the dressing over. Garnish with extra chives.

Pumpkin, Oyster Mushroom and Ricotta Filo Parcels

450 g (1 lb) pumpkin, diced
175 g (6 oz) oyster
  mushrooms
butter for cooking
175 g (6 oz) ricotta cheese
salt and pepper

6 sheets of filo pastry
100 g (4 oz) carrots, peeled
  and chopped
600 ml (1 pint) vegetable
  stock
fresh coriander

1. Sauté the pumpkin and oyster mushrooms separately in butter. (The pumpkin should be soft but not puréed, and keep its shape.)
2. Mix the pumpkin with the ricotta and mushrooms. Season with salt and pepper. Leave until cold, then divide into 6 equal portions.
3. Double each individual layer of filo pastry and brush with melted butter. Wrap the mixture into rectangular parcels. Place in the refrigerator.
4. Cook the carrots in the vegetable stock with coriander to taste. Season lightly. When cooked, purée in a blender, then pass through a sieve.
5. Brush the filo parcels with butter. Bake in the oven at 200°C (400°F) mark 6 for 10 minutes. Serve with the carrot and coriander sauce.

Hazelnut and White Chocolate Torte

75 g (3 oz) caster sugar
75 g (3 oz) butter
50 g (2 oz) ground almonds
100 g (4 oz) ground
  hazelnuts

175 g (6 oz) white
  chocolate,
  grated
4 eggs, separated
icing sugar for dusting

1. Heat the sugar and butter, then remove from the heat when the sugar has dissolved. Add the almonds and hazelnuts, then the grated white chocolate and egg yolks.
2. Whisk the egg whites and fold into the mixture carefully.
3. Line a round 15–18 cm (6–8 inch) flan ring with greaseproof paper and brush with oil; preferably using an open flan ring on a baking sheet. Add the chocolate and nut mixture.
4. Bake in the oven at 200°C (400°F) mark 6 for 12–15 minutes. Dust the torte with icing sugar.
5. Serve warm with crème fraîche and cranberries. For tangy cranberries, take dried cranberries and heat in white wine with sugar until the liquid is absorbed and the consistency is syrupy but slightly sour. The sweetness of the torte, sharpness of the cranberries and the crème fraîche work well together.

BRASSERIE FORTY-FOUR
Leeds

Fresh Pasta with Strips of Chicken, Pesto and Roast Peppers

Salmon Fishcakes with Leaf Spinach

Crisp Apple Pastry with Cinnamon Mascarpone

Serves 4

Fresh Pasta with Strips of Chicken, Pesto and Roast Peppers

300 ml (½ pint) double cream
1 large chicken supreme, very finely sliced
30 ml (2 tbsp) pesto
salt and pepper
350 g (12 oz) fresh tagliatelle

2 red peppers, roasted, peeled and cut into 8 strips
50 g (2 oz) Parmesan cheese, grated

1. Gently heat the cream in a saucepan. Add the chicken strips and cook for 2–3 minutes. Stir in the pesto and season.
2. Cook the pasta in boiling salted water until tender. Divide between 4 warm serving bowls. Pour the sauce and chicken over the pasta. Garnish with strips of red pepper and freshly grated Parmesan. Serve immediately.

Salmon Fishcakes with Leaf Spinach

350 g (12 oz) poached
 salmon, flaked
350 g (12 oz) potato purée
3 eggs
chopped fresh parsley
salt and pepper
175 g (6 oz) tomato flesh,
 diced

2 shallots, skinned and
 diced
50 g (2 oz) capers
virgin olive oil
seasoned flour for coating
450 g (1 lb) spinach,
 washed
25 g (1 oz) butter

1. Mix together the salmon, potato purée, 1 egg, some parsley and seasoning to taste.
2. Bind the diced tomato, shallots, capers, some parsley and olive oil to form a dressing.
3. Divide the salmon mixture into quarters. Roll in flour to coat. Whisk the remaining 2 eggs and use to cover fish cakes.
4. Heat 30 ml (2 tbsp) olive oil in a pan until very hot. Add the fishcakes, making sure they do not touch. Brown on both sides. Finish off in the oven at 220°C (425°F) mark 7 for about 5 minutes.
5. Cook the spinach in a pan with butter until wilted. Season. Place onto 4 warm serving plates.
6. Gently heat the dressing and spoon around the spinach. Place a fishcake on top and serve immediately.

Crisp Apple Pastry with Cinnamon Mascarpone

four Granny Smith apples,
 peeled, cored and thinly
 sliced
four 10 cm (4 inch) thin puff
 pastry rounds
butter

30 ml (2 tbsp) brown sugar
juice of 1 lemon
60 ml (4 tbsp) mascarpone
 cheese
ground cinnamon to taste

1. Fan the apples on to the pastry rounds. Dot with butter, sugar and lemon juice evenly.
2. Bake in the oven at 220–230°C (425–450°F) mark 7–8 for 10 minutes until the sugar has caramelized and serve immediately with quenelles of mascarpone dusted with cinnamon in the centre.

LE CAFE DES AMIS DU VIN
London, WC2

Salad of Warm Wild Mushrooms
Sea Bream with Tagliatelle
Baked Bananas with Orange and Lemon

Serves 4–6

Salad of Warm Wild Mushrooms

450 g (1 lb) oyster
  mushrooms
25 g (1 oz) unsalted butter
1 courgette, cut into julienne
  strips
1 carrot, peeled and cut into
  julienne strips

5 ml (1 tsp) raspberry
  vinegar
salt and pepper
mixed salad leaves, to
  garnish

1. Sauté the mushrooms in the butter, without colouring. Add the courgette and carrot and cook lightly.
2. Add the raspberry vinegar and deglaze. Season to taste.
3. Place on a bed of mixed salad leaves and serve.

Sea Bream with Tagliatelle

2 sea bream, 700–900 g
(1½–2 lb) each
75 g (3 oz) unsalted butter
200 g (7 oz) fresh tagliatelle
600 ml (1 pint) fish stock

25 g (1 oz) plain flour
salt and pepper
2 lemons, quartered
1 bunch of parsley

1. Fillet the fish to provide 4 good sized fillets. Pan fry the fillets in 50 g (2 oz) of the butter until golden brown.
2. Place the pasta in a large saucepan of boiling water and boil for 4 minutes so that the pasta remains firm. Drain.
3. Heat the fish stock in a saucepan. Melt the remaining butter in another pan and blend in the flour to create a roux, do not allow to colour. Gradually add the boiled fish stock to the roux, stirring constantly. Season.
4. Combine the fish sauce with the pasta and gently heat. Put the pasta on serving plates and place the fish on top. Garnish with lemon and parsley.

Baked Bananas with Orange and Lemon

6 firm bananas, peeled
22.5 ml (1½ tbsp) lemon
juice
5 ml (1 tsp) grated orange
rind
45 ml (3 tbsp) dark brown
sugar

pinch of grated nutmeg
1.25 ml (¼ tsp) ground
cinnamon
30 ml (2 tbsp) unsalted
butter, cut into small
cubes
crème fraîche, to serve

1. Cut each banana into 3 pieces and place in a well buttered dish. Sprinkle with lemon juice and grated orange rind.
2. Combine the sugar, nutmeg and cinnamon and sprinkle all over the bananas. Dot with butter.
3. Bake in the oven at 180°C (350°F) mark 4 for 30–45 minutes. Serve hot with generous scoops of crème fraîche.

CAFE DES ARTS
London, NW3

Crostini with Broad Bean, Mint and Lemon Purée
Baked Mackerel Fillets with Avocado and Caper Salsa
Frozen Orange and Ginger Parfait

Serves 4–6

Crostini with Broad Bean, Mint and Lemon Purée

450 g (1 lb) broad beans
extra virgin olive oil
lemon juice

chopped fresh mint
1 ciabatta bread
1 clove of garlic, skinned

1. Cook the broad beans in boiling salted water until tender. Purée in a blender. Drizzle olive oil, lemon juice and chopped fresh mint to taste over the bean purée. (If the purée is very thick, add a little vegetable stock.)
2. The purée can be served warm or made in advance and served at room temperature.
3. Slice the ciabatta bread. Coat each slice with extra virgin olive oil and rub with garlic. Grill and serve warm with the purée. Place a large spoonful of purée on a plate with the crostinis alongside.

Baked Mackerel Fillets with Avocado and Caper Salsa

900 g (2 lb) mackerel fillets
white wine to cover
lemon juice
butter
salt and pepper

Avocado and caper salsa:
1 red pepper, seeded
1 green pepper, seeded

4 tomatoes, skinned
1 chilli, seeded
15 ml (1 tbsp) capers
2 ripe avocados, stoned
1 red onion, skinned
1 clove of garlic, skinned
extra virgin olive oil
lemon juice

1. Place the mackerel fillets in a baking dish and cover with white wine, lemon juice, a little butter and seasoning to taste.
2. Bake in the oven at 190°C (375°F) mark 5 until firm.
3. For the salsa, finely dice all the ingredients and mix together. Coat with extra virgin olive oil and lemon juice. Serve a large spoonful on a plate and place a mackerel fillet over it.

Frozen Orange and Ginger Parfait

600 ml (1 pint) freshly
  squeezed orange juice
grated zest of 2 oranges
100 g (4 oz) fresh root
  ginger, peeled

8 egg yolks
225 g (8 oz) sugar
900 ml (1½ pints) whipping
  cream, lightly whipped

1. Combine the orange juice, orange zest, puréed fresh ginger (puréed in the blender with a little of the fresh orange juice) in a pan. Bring to the boil.
2. Whisk the egg yolks with the sugar until thick and pale. When the juice boils, pour onto the egg mixture and beat hard to avoid curdling. Put back into the pan and cook very gently until it thickens slightly.
3. Transfer the orange mixture to a bowl and put in the refrigerator to cool. When cold, fold in the semi-whipped whipping cream.
4. Line a loaf tin with cling film, pour in the mixture and freeze. Take it out a few minutes before serving.
5. Serve with a thin sauce made by simmering orange juice, lemon juice and sugar until just syrupy, with thin strips of orange zest added at the last minute.

CAFE FLO GROUP
see Restaurant List for locations

Warm Lentil Salad
Pike with Herb Butter
Pears Belle Hélène

Serves 4–6

Warm Lentil Salad

300 g (11 oz) green lentils
15 g (½ oz) butter
2 onions, skinned and
  coarsely chopped
3 cloves of garlic, skinned
  and halved
sprig of fresh thyme
1 bay leaf
1 bottle of dry white wine

Vinaigrette:
90 ml (6 tbsp) olive oil
30 ml (2 tbsp) sherry
  vinegar
15 ml (1 tbsp) strong
  mustard
30 ml (2 tbsp) finely
  chopped chives
salt and pepper

1. Pick over the lentils, rinse well and soak in warm water if necessary.
2. Melt the butter in a flameproof casserole over a moderate heat. Add the onions, garlic, thyme and bay leaf and stir for 2 minutes.
3. Mix in the drained lentils, then pour on the wine and bring to the boil. Lower the heat, cover and simmer for about 40 minutes or until tender.
4. To make the vinaigrette, whisk together all the ingredients. Season to taste.
5. Drain the cooked lentils and put them in a serving bowl, discarding the thyme and bay leaf.
6. Pour over the vinaigrette while the lentils are still hot. Stir and leave to cool slightly.

Pike with Herb Butter

1 whole pike, 1.35 kg (3 lb)
  in weight
juice of 1 lemon
salt and pepper
75 g (3 oz) butter

2 shallots, skinned and
  chopped
45 ml (3 tbsp) chopped
  fresh parsley
10 tarragon leaves, chopped

1. Remove the head from the pike. Clean, scale and wash the fish. Slit it lengthways to remove the backbone. Sprinkle the insides of the pike with lemon juice, salt and pepper.
2. Grease a deep ovenproof dish with some of the butter and spread the shallots over the bottom. Put the opened out pike on top of the shallots, flesh side down. Make 6–7 slashes in the skin with a sharp knife.
3. Work the remaining butter in a bowl until soft, then add chopped parsley and tarragon. Force small quantities of this mixture into the slashes in the skin. Bake in the oven at 200°C (400°F) mark 6 for 30 minutes, basting occasionally.

Pears Belle Hélène

6 Williams pears
50 g (2 oz) caster sugar
125 g (4½ oz) plain
  chocolate, broken into
  small pieces

25 g (1 oz) butter
vanilla ice cream

1. Peel the pears but leave them whole and do not remove the stalks.
2. Dissolve the sugar in 250 ml (8 fl oz) water in a saucepan. Poach the pears gently in this syrup for about 20 minutes or until quite tender, turning them about halfway through. Drain and chill.
3. Meanwhile, boil the syrup rapidly to reduce by half. Melt the chocolate in the syrup, followed by the butter and stir until the sauce is smooth and creamy. Remove immediately from the heat.
4. To serve, put a small scoop of ice cream into a thoroughly chilled glass, add one chilled pear and coat immediately with hot chocolate sauce.

CAFE ROYAL BRASSERIE
London, W1

Baked Stuffed Mushrooms with Warm Olive Oil and Balsamic Vinegar Sauce

Braised Knuckle of Lamb with Roast Garlic and Root Vegetables

Strawberry Soup with Crème Fraîche and Vanilla Ice Cream

Serves 6

Baked Stuffed Mushrooms with Warm Olive Oil and Balsamic Vinegar Sauce

6 large grilling mushrooms, 10–12.5 cm (4–5 inch) diameter
2 courgettes, thinly sliced
2 onions, skinned and sliced
olive oil for cooking
3 cloves of garlic, skinned and crushed
25 g (1 oz) sun-dried tomatoes
3 tomatoes, seeded and diced
15 ml (1 tbsp) chopped basil
salt and pepper

2 packets Mozzarella cheese, sliced
fresh diced tomatoes and basil leaves, to garnish

Vinaigrette:
75 ml (3 fl oz) cooking juices from the mushrooms
75 ml (3 fl oz) balsamic vinegar
275 ml (9 fl oz) virgin olive oil
7.5 ml (½ tbsp) chopped fresh basil

1. Clean and peel the mushrooms. Blanch the courgette slices in boiling salted water for 10 seconds.
2. Cook the onions in olive oil very slowly until golden and soft. Add the garlic, sun-dried and fresh tomatoes and the basil. Season to taste.
3. Place this mix on top of the mushrooms (black gills side up). Cover with the courgette slices, then the Mozzarella slices.
4. Place the mushrooms in a baking dish. Sprinkle with olive oil and salt and pepper. Cook in the oven at 200°C (400°F) mark 6 until golden brown.
5. To serve, mix the ingredients for the vinaigrette in a pan. Heat slightly, then pour round the baked mushrooms. Garnish with fresh diced tomatoes and basil leaves.

Braised Knuckle of Lamb with Roast Garlic and Root Vegetables

6 shanks of lamb
salt and pepper
45 ml (3 tbsp) oil
450 g (1 lb) lamb bones
2 onions, skinned and
  chopped
2 carrots, peeled and
  chopped
2 sticks of celery, chopped
1 bulb of garlic, skinned and
  chopped
2 tomatoes, seeded
30 ml (2 tbsp) tomato purée
1 glass of dry white wine
1.7 litres (3 pints) veal or
  lamb stock
1 bay leaf

1 sprig of thyme
1 sprig of rosemary
peppercorns
coriander seeds
1 piece of smoked bacon
  rind

Garnish:
2 bulbs of garlic
olive oil
900 g (2 lb) new potatoes
900 g (2 lb) mixed root
  vegetables, such as
  potatoes, turnips, swede,
  carrots, celeriac, parsnips
butter for cooking
chopped fresh parsley

1. Sprinkle the shanks with seasoning. Heat the oil in a flameproof casserole and brown the lamb. Set aside.
2. Brown the lamb bones in the same casserole. Add the chopped vegetables and cook until soft and golden brown. Add the tomatoes and tomato purée and very slowly cook for 5 minutes.
3. Deglaze with the white wine, add the stock, herbs, some peppercorns and coriander seeds. Put the shanks back into the casserole with the smoked bacon rind. Bring to the boil, skim and adjust seasoning. Braise in the oven at 170°C (325°F) mark 3 for about 1½–1¾ hours or until tender.
4. Lift out the knuckles and keep warm. Reduce the stock, adjust seasoning and strain over the knuckles. Keep hot.
5. For the garnish, break the garlic into cloves and cook for 10 minutes in lots of salted water. Drain and gently roast in olive oil until golden brown.
6. Peel and cut the root vegetables into bite size sticks or cubes. Blanch in salted water, then slightly sauté them in butter.
7. To serve, arrange all the vegetables and roasted garlic round the shanks and pour the sauce over. Sprinkle with chopped parsley and serve with garlic bread, if liked.

Strawberry Soup with Crème Fraîche and Vanilla Ice Cream

Select the summer berries according to availability and season. Frozen fruits are fine to use.

450 g (1 lb) mixed summer berries, such as strawberries, raspberries, blueberries, blackberries, tayberries, red, white and blackcurrants
350 g (12 oz) caster sugar
300 ml (½ pint) double cream

600 ml (1 pint) crème fraîche
juice from 2 lemons
1 glass of Sauternes (optional)
icing sugar (optional)
berries, to decorate
mint
vanilla ice cream, to serve

1. Place the berries, sugar and 600 ml (1 pint) water in a saucepan and cook for 5 minutes.
2. Cool, then purée in a blender for a few seconds. Strain through a fine sieve. Chill.
3. Mix in the cream, crème fraîche, lemon juice and optional glass of Sauternes. Add sugar to taste.
4. To serve, put a cupful of soup in a soup bowl, place a scoop of vanilla ice cream in the middle and decorate with berries, icing sugar and mint.

CAFE ROUGE GROUP
see Restaurant List for locations

Duck, Bacon and Avocado Salad
Poached Chicken in Cream and Ginger Sauce
Crème Brûlée with Strawberries

Serves 4–6

Duck, Bacon and Avocado Salad

100 g (4 oz) smoked bacon, rinded
1 ripe avocado
100 g (4 oz) new potatoes, scrubbed
1 male duck breast, about 200 g (7 oz), trimmed
½ curly endive, 250 g (9 oz)
½ lollo rosso, 250 g (9 oz)
½ oakleaf lettuce, 250 g (9 oz)
45 ml (3 tbsp) cider vinegar

Vinaigrette:
salt and pepper
Dijon mustard
juice of ½ lemon
50 ml (3½ tbsp) wine vinegar
100 ml (4 fl oz) olive oil

1. Cut the bacon into lardons (small strips). Place in a saucepan, cover with water and blanch for 2 minutes. Refresh and drain.
2. Halve the avocado lengthways, remove the stone and peel. Dice.
3. Place the new potatoes in a pan of cold seasoned water. Cook for about 20 minutes until soft.
4. For the vinaigrette, mix together the salt, pepper, mustard, lemon juice and wine vinegar. Whisk in the olive oil slowly.
5. Heat a frying pan until quite hot and place the seasoned duck breast, fat side down, in the pan. When the fat has browned, turn the breast over and seal the other side. Remove and leave to cool. Cut into thin slices.
6. Trim, wash and dry the salads. Toss the endive and oakleaf in the vinaigrette and arrange on a plate. Surround with lollo rosso.
7. In a frying pan, sauté the lardons and sliced duck breast. Place neatly on the mixed leaves and deglaze the pan with the cider vinegar, reducing the vinegar by half. Spoon over the salad. Slice the warm new potatoes and place around the duck and top with the avocado. Serve immediately.

Poached Chicken in Cream and Ginger Sauce

2 shallots, skinned and finely
   chopped
knob of unsalted butter
50 g (2 oz) fresh root ginger,
   peeled and grated
100 ml (4 fl oz) white wine
300 ml (½ pint) double
   cream

125 g (4½ oz) chilled
   unsalted butter, cubed
600 ml (1 pint) chicken
   stock
bouquet garni
4 chicken breasts, 150 g
   (5 oz) each, trimmed

1. Fry the shallots in a saucepan with a knob of butter until tender. Add the ginger and fry for a further 30 seconds. Pour in the white wine and reduce by two thirds. Add the cream and reduce until it starts to turn yellow.
2. Remove from the heat and when it has stopped boiling, add the butter, slowly whisking all the time. (At this stage, do not re-boil the sauce.) Keep warm.
3. Heat the chicken stock with the bouquet garni. When simmering remove any fat from the surface with a ladle. Place the chicken breasts in the stock and cook for about 6 minutes or until firm to the touch.
4. Remove the chicken and dry with a clean cloth. Arrange neatly on a serving dish and coat with the sauce. Serve with seasonal vegetables.

Crème Brûlée with Strawberries

4 eggs
600 ml (1 pint) double
   cream
90 g (3½ oz) sugar

vanilla essence
6 strawberries, sliced
icing sugar

1. Whisk the eggs, cream and sugar together and add a few drops of vanilla essence.
2. Place a couple of slices of strawberry in each ramekin and pour on the egg mixture. Cook in a bain marie in the oven at 170°C (325°F) mark 3 until set.
3. Remove from the oven, coat lightly with icing sugar and glaze under the grill. Serve immediately.

DAN'S
London, SW3

Warm Salad of Duck Livers
Navarin of Lamb
Normandy Apple Tart

Serves 4–6

Warm Salad of Duck Livers

1 curly endive or 700 g
** (1½ lb) spinach**
vinaigrette dressing
4 duck livers, trimmed
** and halved**

salt and pepper
30 ml (2 tbsp) oil for frying
30 ml (2 tbsp) wine vinegar
30 ml (2 tbsp) milk

1. Wash the greens, dry thoroughly. Shortly before serving, add vinaigrette to the leaves to soften.
2. Place livers in bowl 3 hours before serving, soaking in lightly salted milk to cover. Rinse livers under running tap water until water runs clear. Drain but do not pat dry.
3. Season the livers with salt and pepper. Heat the oil until very hot and sauté the livers over a very high heat for 1–2 minutes on each side. Place the livers on the salad.
4. Discard any fat remaining in the pan and add the vinegar. Bring to the boil to deglaze the pan, pour over the leaves and mix well.

Navarin of Lamb

900 g (2 lb) shoulder or
  boned breast of lamb,
  cubed
butter and olive oil for
  cooking
225 g (8 oz) onions, skinned
  and sliced
225 g (8 oz) carrots, peeled
  and chopped
225 g (8 oz) turnips, peeled
  and chopped
2 sticks of celery, chopped
225 g (8 oz) flageolet beans
bouquet garni
salt and pepper
15 ml (1 tbsp) cornflour
15 ml (1 tbsp) tomato purée

1. Place the lamb in a flameproof casserole and brown in butter and olive oil for 5 minutes over a gentle heat. Add the onions, then the root vegetables and celery.
2. Pour in enough water (half way up), cover and cook gently for 20 minutes, stirring occasionally. Check the liquid to make sure the dish is not drying out, then add the beans and bouquet garni. Season and bring to a gentle boil, cover and cook for another 15 minutes. Turn the meat and vegetables into a serving dish.
3. Mix the cornflour with 250 ml (8 fl oz) water and the tomato purée until smooth. Make the cooking juices up to about 300 ml (½ pint) with water, then add the tomato and cornflour mixture. Bring to the boil, stirring until the mixture thickens, then pour over the meat. The dish should be quite liquid as it is really a stew.

Normandy Apple Tart

3–4 ripe dessert apples

Pâte brisée:
200 g (6½ oz) plain flour
100 g (3½ oz) butter
1 egg yolk
20 ml (¾ tsp) salt

Frangipane:
100 g (3½ oz) butter

100 g (3½ oz) caster sugar
1 egg, beaten
1 egg yolk
10 ml (2 tsp) Calvados or Kirsch
100 g (3½ oz) whole blanched almonds, ground
30 ml (2 tbsp) flour

1. For the pâte brisée, sift the flour onto a board and make a large well in the centre. Pound the butter to soften it slightly. Place the butter, egg yolk, salt and 45 ml (2½ tbsp) water in the well and work together with the fingertips until partly mixed. Gradually work in the flour, using the fingertips to pull the dough into large crumbs. If the crumbs are dry, sprinkle over more water. Press the dough firmly together, it should be soft but not sticky. Wrap the pâte brisée and chill for at least 30 minutes.
2. Heat the oven to 200°C (400°F) mark 6 and place a baking sheet in the oven to heat.
3. Roll out the dough and use to line a 25–27 cm (10–11 inch) tart tin. Prick lightly with a fork, flute the edges and chill again until firm.
4. For the frangipane, cream the butter, gradually beat in the sugar and continue beating until the mixture is light and soft. Gradually add the egg and yolk, then Calvados or Kirsch. Stir in the ground almonds and flour. Pour the frangipane into the chilled pastry case, spreading it evenly.
5. Peel the apples, halve them and core. Cut them crossways in very thin slices. Arrange the apple slices on the frangipane to make the spokes of a wheel, keeping the slices together. Press them down gently until they touch the pastry dough base.
6. Bake the pie on the hot baking sheet near the bottom of the oven for 10–15 minutes until the pastry dough is beginning to brown. Reduce the oven temperature to 180°C (350°F) mark 4 and continue cooking for 15–20 minutes.
7. Ten minutes before the end of cooking, sprinkle the tart with caster sugar and continue cooking until the sugar melts and caramelises slightly.

DEL BUONGUSTAIO
London, SW15

Spinach and Artichoke Rice Torte
Guinea Fowl with Italian Bacon and Sausage
Iced Mascarpone Cream

Serves 4–6

Spinach and Artichoke Rice Torte

450 g (1 lb) fresh spinach,
  washed
salt and pepper
4 medium globe artichokes
1 medium onion, skinned
  and finely chopped

40 ml (8 tsp) olive oil
100 g (4 oz) arborio rice
3 eggs, beaten
100 g (4 oz) grated
  Parmesan cheese
100 ml (4 fl oz) milk

1. Cook the spinach in boiling salted water for 10 minutes (if you
   put the spinach in when the water is already boiling, it will retain
   its colour).
2. Clean the artichokes by removing the hard stringy bits and the
   outer leaves. Boil in a separate pan of boiling water for 10–15
   minutes (until a fork will almost penetrate). Chop both the
   spinach and artichoke finely and leave to one side.
3. Fry the onion slowly in 30 ml (6 tsp) of the oil for 10 minutes.
   Add the chopped spinach and artichokes and cook for a further
   2–3 minutes.
4. Meanwhile, cook the rice in boiling salted water until 'al dente' –
   about 15 minutes. Drain the rice and add the vegetable mixture.
   Then add the beaten eggs, Parmesan cheese, milk and a dash of
   salt and pepper.
5. Oil a baking tin or dish with the remaining olive oil, then pour in
   the mixture.
6. Cook in the oven at 180°C (350°F) mark 4 for 1 hour. Leave to
   cool a little and serve cut in slices on tossed leaves and herbs.

Guinea Fowl with Italian Bacon and Sausage

1 kg (2¼ lb) guinea fowl
25–50 g (1–2 oz) dried
  porcini mushrooms,
  depending on taste
225 g (8 oz) spring onions,
  trimmed and finely chopped
100 g (4 oz) Italian pancetta
  bacon, roughly chopped

40 g (1½ oz) butter
10 ml (2 tsp) plain flour
500 ml (17 fl oz) Merlot
  wine
salt and pepper
250 g (9 oz) Italian fresh
  sausage, roughly chopped

1. Clean and wash the guinea fowl, then cut into 8 pieces. Soak the dried porcini mushrooms in warm water for about 10 minutes.
2. In a large pan, gently sauté the onion and pancetta bacon in the butter for a few minutes. Roll the guinea fowl pieces in flour, then add them to the onion and pancetta bacon and sauté until lightly browned. Add the wine and salt and pepper to taste. Cover and cook over a moderate heat for about 1 hour.
3. Remove the guinea fowl pieces and leave them to one side. Put the sauce back over a moderate heat and add the mushrooms and sausage. Cook for another 20 minutes.
4. Finally add the guinea fowl to the sauce and cook over a very low heat for a further 5 minutes. This dish can be served on its own or with freshly made soft polenta.

Iced Mascarpone Cream

4 eggs, separated
250 g (9 oz) icing sugar
1 small glass of Galliano or
  Aurum

350 g (12 oz) mascarpone
  cheese
500 ml (17 fl oz) fresh
  whipped cream

1. Beat the egg whites. In a separate bowl, beat together the egg yolks, icing sugar and liqueur.
2. Add the mascarpone to this mixture and, when well mixed in, add the egg whites and whipped cream. Pour this mixture into a rectangular container. Freeze for 3 hours.
3. Remove from the freezer 10 minutes before serving and serve cut in thick slices. Serve with braised fresh fruits or with melted dark chocolate.

DELL'UGO
London, W1

Caramelised Chicory Tart
Marinated Red Mullet with Stuffed Peppers
Fresh Figs with Parmesan and Rocket

Serves 6

Caramelised Chicory Tart

8 heads of chicory	salt and pepper
600 ml (1 pint) orange juice	100 g (4 oz) butter
30 ml (2 tbsp) chopped fresh coriander	100 g (4 oz) caster sugar
	100 g (4 oz) puff pastry
30 ml (2 tbsp) chopped fresh mint	

1. Braise the chicory whole in the orange juice, herbs and salt and pepper until soft, about 25 minutes. Drain well and refrigerate overnight to dry out thoroughly. Halve the chicory lengthwise.
2. Spread the butter over the base of a straight-edged oven and flameproof dish. Sprinkle the sugar over and pack the chicory on top, cut side down.
3. Roll out the pastry 1 cm (½ inch) thick. Cover the chicory with the pastry, tucking it in at the edges. Place the dish on top of the cooker until the butter and sugar begins to caramelise at the edges.
4. Prick the pastry. Bake in the oven at 220°C (425°F) mark 7 for about 20 minutes or until the pastry is golden brown. Invert and serve warm or cold.

Marinated Red Mullet with Stuffed Peppers

juice of 4 limes, plus grated
   zest of 1 lime
1 chilli, chopped
1 clove of garlic, skinned
   and finely chopped
1 red onion, skinned and
   chopped
5 ml (1 tsp) caster sugar

6 red mullet fillets, scaled
   but not skinned
100 g (4 oz) wild rice
6 red peppers
30 ml (2 tbsp) chopped
   black olives
pepper
olive oil

1. Combine the lime juice, zest, chilli, garlic, onion and sugar in a
   shallow dish. Lay the fish in the dish, refrigerate and marinate,
   turning regularly, for 1–2 hours.
2. Meanwhile, cook the wild rice. Grill the peppers until the skins
   turn black. Seal them in a polythene bag for 10 minutes to make
   it easier to remove the skin. Core and remove the seeds. Fill the
   peppers with wild rice.
3. Grill the fish and arrange with the peppers on a serving platter.
   Scatter with chopped olives and black pepper, and drizzle over a
   little olive oil.

Fresh Figs with Parmesan and Rocket

6 fresh figs
100 g (4 oz) piece Parmesan
   cheese
rocket leaves

salad dressing using
   balsamic vinegar and
   olive oil

1. Quarter the figs. Shave the Parmesan into broad curls with a
   potato peeler.
2. Arrange the figs on a platter with the Parmesan shavings. Add
   the rocket and spoon over the dressing.

FREDERICK'S
London, N1

Briottini
Mississippi Cat Fish with Crab
Pears in Cinnamon Wine

Serves 4

Briottini

4 slices of brioche, 1 cm
  (½ inch) thick 7.5 cm
  (3 inch) diameter
olive oil
100 g (4 oz) mascarpone
  cheese
100 g (4 oz) cream cheese
20 ml (4 tsp) chopped fresh
  chives

juice of ½ lemon
salt and pepper
200 g (7 oz) smoked
  salmon,
  thinly sliced
few seasonal salad leaves
salad dressing, made using
  balsamic vinegar
sprig of dill, to garnish

1. Brush the brioche slices with a little olive oil. Grill both sides.
2. Mix together the mascarpone and cream cheese. Add the chives, lemon juice and seasoning to taste. Spoon the cheese mixture onto the brioche slices, forming a slight dome towards the centre.
3. Arrange the smoked salmon tastefully on the slices to cover most of it. Garnish with a sprig of dill and arrange a few salad leaves with balsamic vinegar dressing on the side.

Mississippi Cat Fish with Crab

four 150 g (5 oz) fresh
  cat fish fillets
200 g (7 oz) fresh crab meat
  sprinkled with sesame oil
salt and pepper
Cajun spices with a touch of
  water

clarified butter for sprinkling
200 g (7 oz) mixed carrots,
  courgettes and leeks

1. With a thin bladed knife, open each fish fillet to form a pocket.
   Fill with crab meat. Brush Cajun spices over the fish.
2. Sprinkle with clarified butter. Bake in the oven at 180°C (350°F)
   mark 4 for about 10 minutes.
3. Cut the carrots, courgettes and leeks into long thin strips to
   make vegetable spaghetti. Serve the fish on a bed of the vegetables. You can serve this with a light creamy crab sauce or a light
   butter sauce with spring onions.

Pears in Cinnamon Wine

4 large round pears
4 scoops of calvados ice
  cream (optional)
4 soup spoons thick crème
  fraîche
mint leaves, to decorate

Syrup:
1 litre (1¾ pints) red wine
2 cinnamon sticks
1 bay leaf
150 g (5 oz) caster sugar
1 clove
peel of 1 orange
peel of 1 lemon

1. Put all the syrup ingredients in a pan and bring to the boil. Peel
   the pears, leaving the stalks on if preferred, and place into the
   simmering syrup.
2. Cook the pears until soft, about 20 minutes. Leave them overnight in the syrup. Remove the pears and reduce the syrup until
   it reaches the desired consistency.
3. Cut a little slice from the bottom of each pear to allow them to sit
   on their bases. Coat each pear with a spoonful of syrup. Serve
   with a spoonful of calvados ice cream and crème fraîche. Decorate with fresh mint leaves.

GILBERTS
London, SW7

Lord Queensberry's Special
Buckwheat Crêpes with Mushrooms and Soured Cream
Iced Lemon Soufflé

Serves 4–6

Lord Queensberry's Special

Marinated kipper fillets so-called because Lord Queensberry was partial to them.

450 g (1 lb) best quality kipper fillets (frozen ones are fine)
lemon juice
olive oil
10 ml (2 tsp) finely chopped shallot

20 ml (4 tsp) finely chopped fresh parsley
freshly ground black pepper
ground sea salt to taste, if necessary

1. Slice the kippers on the diagonal (this is easier if they are well chilled or partially frozen) to about the thickness of a £1 coin. Cover completely with lemon juice overnight (minimum 12 hours).
2. Drain thoroughly and moisten generously with olive oil. Add the shallot, parsley and seasoning to taste. Serve chilled with thinly sliced brown bread and butter.

Buckwheat Crêpes with Mushrooms and Soured Cream

Crêpe batter:
40 g (1½ oz) butter
350 ml (12 fl oz) milk
5 ml (1 tsp) sugar
5 ml (1 tsp) salt
40 g (1½ oz) buckwheat flour
65 g (2½ oz) plain flour
2 large eggs, size 1 or 2
30 ml (2 tbsp) oil
75–100 ml (3–4 fl oz) lager

Filling:
2 onions, skinned and finely chopped

50 g (2 oz) butter
1 clove of garlic, skinned and crushed
700 g (1½ lb) mushrooms, sliced
300 ml (½ pint) soured cream
lemon juice
salt and pepper
chopped fresh parsley
chopped fresh chives

1. For the batter, place all the ingredients in a blender. Blend thoroughly. Leave for at least 20 minutes before making the crêpes.
2. To make the crêpes, heat a non-stick or heavy frying pan and pour in 30–45 ml (2–3 tbsp) batter. Cook for 2–3 minutes, flip over and cook the second side for 2–3 minutes.
3. For the filling, soften the onions in the butter. Add the garlic and soften. Stir in the mushrooms and cook until just tender.
4. Remove from the heat and add enough soured cream to bind the mixture. Season with lemon juice, salt, pepper and parsley.
5. Fill each crêpe with 30 ml (2 tbsp) of the mushroom mixture, then fold or roll neatly. Brush with butter and reheat gently under the grill or in the oven. Add chives to the remaining soured cream. Season lightly and serve warmed or chilled with the hot crêpes.

Iced Lemon Soufflé

3 eggs, separated
100 g (4 oz) caster sugar
7.5 ml (½ tbsp) lemon
  zest
175 ml (6 fl oz) double
  cream

7.5 ml (½ tbsp) powdered
  gelatine
65 ml (2½ fl oz) lemon juice
  or more to taste
1 egg white

1. Whisk the egg yolks, sugar and lemon zest together until pale and fluffy. Add the cream slowly, whisking continuously until thick.
2. Dissolve the gelatine in the lemon juice and allow to cool. Mix into the lemon mixture quickly and thoroughly.
3. Beat the egg whites until stiff but not dry and fold them in gently. Freeze the mixture in a 1 litre (1½ pint) container. A loaf tin is ideal as the soufflé can be turned out and sliced to serve.

GRILL ST QUENTIN
London, SW3

Onion Soup with Cheese Topping
Ox Cheek Stew
Chocolate Slab

Serves 4–6

Onion Soup with Cheese Topping

50 g (2 oz) salted butter
50 ml (2 fl oz) vegetable oil
1 kg (2 lb) onions, skinned
   and finely sliced
1 clove of garlic, skinned
   and finely chopped
40 g (1½ oz) plain flour

2.3 litres (4 pints) beef
   stock
salt and pepper
1 small French loaf
175–225 g (6–8 oz) Gruyère
   cheese, grated
croûtons, to serve

1. Heat the butter and oil in a heavy-based saucepan and gently fry the onions and garlic over a low heat, stirring all the time, until the onion is a dark golden brown colour, but has not burned.
2. Add the flour and mix well. Leave to cook in the fat for no more than a few seconds. Add the stock and bring to the boil, stirring frequently. Reduce the heat and simmer gently until reduced in volume by a third. (At this stage the onion will have become very soft.)
3. Check the seasoning, if necessary adding a little salt and pepper. Care should be taken with the seasoning, particularly if stock cubes have been used.
4. Slice the French loaf into rounds about 0.5 cm (¼ inch) thick. Toast them under a grill.
5. To serve, place the soup into ovenproof soup bowls. Put some grated cheese into the bowl with the soup, followed by enough croûtons to cover most of the surface of the soup in the bowl. Add another more generous helping of grated cheese.

6. Place the soup bowls in the oven at 220°C (425°F) mark 7 until the cheese has melted and turned golden brown.

Variations: For a stronger tasting finish, a little grated Parmesan may be added into the final layer of grated cheese.
About 300 ml (½ pint) beef stock may be replaced with the same amount of white wine.

Ox Cheek Stew

1–1.5 kg (2½–3 lb) ox cheek   25 g (1 oz) flour
salt and pepper   600 ml (1 pint) light ale
50 g (2 oz) lard   1.1 litres (2 pints) beef stock
450 g (1 lb) onions, skinned   bouquet garni
   and thinly sliced

1. Clean and trim the meat, leaving it in large manageable pieces. Season.
2. Melt the lard in a frying pan and brown the meat on both sides. Remove and put to one side. Add the onions to the pan and fry gently to soften and brown. Add the flour, stir it in well and allow to cook for a few seconds. Stir in the ale and bring to the boil, stirring all the time.
3. Pour in the stock and bring back to the boil, skimming off and discarding any fat and scum rising to the surface. Add the bouquet garni and the browned meat. Bring back to the boil, skimming again if necessary.
4. The stew can be cooked on top of the cooker or in the oven. If cooked on top of the cooker, it is necessary to put a cover on and to drastically reduce the heat so that it just ticks over. It is important to check it occasionally to make sure that the meat does not overcook, and that it does not burn. If cooking in the oven, again it must be covered and put into the oven at 170°C (325°F) mark 3 until the meat is tender.
5. When the meat is cooked, check the sauce for seasoning, if necessary adding a little salt and pepper.

Note: When braising or stewing meat in this way, it is impossible to estimate how long it will take; the only sure way is to take a medium-sized piece out and try it.

Chocolate Slab

350 g (12 oz) bitter
  chocolate
100 g (4 oz) cocoa powder
225 g (8 oz) flaked almonds
caster sugar
slices of orange, halved

sugar syrup
600 ml (1 pint) double
  cream
50 ml (2 fl oz) Grand
  Marnier

1. Melt the chocolate and cocoa powder in a bain marie.
2. Sprinkle the almonds with caster sugar and toast under the grill
   or in the oven. To crystalise the orange slices, dip in the syrup.
3. Bring the cream to the boil. When boiling, mix with the melted
   chocolate, then stir with a whisk. Add the crystallised orange
   slices, almonds and Grand Marnier. Spoon into a terrine and
   freeze. Leave for 2 hours before cutting.

HILAIRE
London, SW7

Vinaigrette of Broccoli, Avocado and Anchovies
Braised Pork with Gremolata and Saffron Risotto
Orange Mousse

Serves 4–6

Vinaigrette of Broccoli, Avocado and Anchovies

1 head of broccoli
1 large avocado
a few leaves of rocket
vinaigrette

16 marinated anchovies
a piece of good Parmesan
  cheese

1. Cook the broccoli in a pan of boiling salted water until just tender. Drain and leave to cool in a bowl.
2. Halve, stone, peel and slice the avocado. Add to the broccoli with the rocket leaves.
3. Dress the mixture with vinaigrette and add the anchovies. Heap individual portions in the centre of a plate.
4. Shave the Parmesan thinly with a potato peeler and place the shavings on the top of each mound.

Braised Pork with Gremolata and Saffron Risotto

arachide oil for frying
1.4 kg (3 lb) boneless shoulder of pork, trimmed and cubed
salt and pepper
4 shallots, skinned and diced
1 large carrot, peeled and diced
2 sticks of celery, diced
1 leek, washed and diced
4 cloves of garlic, skinned and crushed
1 large glass of white wine
100 g (4 oz) passata or one 225 g (8 oz) can of tomatoes
1.1 litres (2 pints) chicken stock
thyme, parsley stalks and 2 bay leaves

Risotto:
600 ml (1 pint) chicken stock with a good pinch of saffron
6 shallots, skinned and finely chopped
200 g (7 oz) risotto rice

Gremolata:
4 cloves of garlic, skinned and crushed
finely grated rind of 1 lemon
1 bunch of flat parsley, finely chopped

1. Heat the oil in a frying pan and seal the pork cubes. Season the pork with salt and pepper and place it in a large saucepan.
2. Sweat the vegetables in the same frying pan but do not colour. Pour in the white wine and continue cooking until the volume is reduced by half.
3. Transfer the wine and vegetables to the saucepan with the pork. Add the passata or canned tomatoes, the chicken stock and herbs. Top up with sufficient cold water to cover. Bring to the boil, skim and simmer for about 1 hour.
4. For the risotto, bring the chicken stock and saffron to the boil, then blend. Sweat the shallots in a saucepan with a little oil but do not colour. Add the rice and stock and season with salt and pepper. Cook slowly on top of the cooker for 15 minutes.
5. For the gremolata, mix the garlic, grated lemon rind and chopped parsley together.
6. Remove the pork pieces from the pan and keep warm. Pass the liquid and vegetables through a sieve, then reduce the juices until they thicken slightly. Return the pork to the sauce and stir in the gremolata. Serve with the risotto on the side.

Orange Mousse

600 ml (1 pint) milk
1 vanilla pod
8 egg yolks
grated rind of 3 oranges
175 g (6 oz) sugar
5 leaves of gelatine, soaked
  in water

juice of 6 oranges
600 ml (1 pint) double
  cream
zest of 3 oranges, cut into
  thin strips
about 60 ml (4 tbsp) orange
  marmalade

1. Simmer the milk with the vanilla pod and allow to infuse.
2. Mix the egg yolks, grated orange rind and sugar together. Add the milk and cook gently until they form a thick custard. Strain.
3. Add the gelatine and all but a little of the orange juice. Leave to set.
4. Whip the cream to a ribbon stage (slightly thick) and fold it into the custard when it is just about to set. Pour into ramekin dishes and leave to continue setting.
5. Blanch the orange zest. Warm some marmalade with a little orange juice, add the blanched zest and leave to cool. When cool, pour a little sauce on top of the mousse and serve.

LE MARCHE NOIR
Edinburgh

Leek and Onion Tart
Wood Pigeon with Honey and Chestnut Sauce
Duo of Poached Pear in Red and White Wine

Serves 4

Leek and Onion Tart

2 leeks, cleaned, washed
  and diced
50 g (2 oz) onions, skinned
  and finely chopped
50 g (2 oz) butter
4 eggs, beaten
300 ml (½ pint) cream
salt and pepper
salad leaves, to garnish

Shortcrust pastry:
150 g (5 oz) plain flour
50 g (2 oz) butter
45 ml (3 tbsp) cream

1. For the shortcrust pastry, mix together the flour and butter. Add the cream and blend until the mixture comes together. Allow to stand in the refrigerator for 20 minutes.
2. Lightly sauté the leeks and onions in the butter, then leave to cool. Mix together the eggs and cream. Season.
3. Roll out the pastry thinly and use to line greased individual tart tins. Bake blind in the oven at 170°C (325°F) mark 3 for about 10 minutes.
4. Place the leek and onion mixture into the tart tins and pour the eggs and cream mixture on top. Bake for a further 10 minutes. Garnish with salad leaves and serve.

Wood Pigeon with Honey and Chestnut Sauce

4 wood pigeon
50 g (2 oz) shallots, skinned
   and finely chopped
100 g (4 oz) chestnuts,
   finely chopped

50 g (2 oz) butter
100 ml (4 fl oz) whisky
10 ml (2 tsp) honey
salt and pepper
vegetable oil for cooking

1. Remove the breasts from the pigeons to leave the carcasses.
   Roast the carcasses in the oven at 170°C (325°F) mark 3 for 10
   minutes until brown.
2. When roasted, put the carcasses in a pan, cover with 600 ml
   (1 pint) cold water and bring to the boil. Reduce by half. This is
   used as the stock for the chestnut and honey sauce.
3. Sauté the shallots and chestnuts in the butter for a few minutes.
   Add the whisky and flame. Stir in the pigeon stock and reduce
   by half again. Add the honey and seasoning to finish the sauce.
4. Season the wood pigeon breasts and sauté in a little oil and butter for about 10 minutes. Once cooked, slice the meat onto
   plates, coat with the sauce and serve.

Duo of Poached Pear in Red and White Wine

15 ml (1 tbsp) sugar
pinch of ground cinnamon
juice of 2 lemons
¼ bottle of red wine
¼ bottle of white wine

4 pears
segments of 1 orange
zest of 1 orange
75 g (3 oz) halved hazelnuts

1. Place half the quantities of sugar, cinnamon, lemon juice and
   300 ml (½ pint) water into 2 separate pans. Add the red wine to
   one pan and white wine to the other.
2. Peel and core the pears, putting 2 into each pan. Bring to the boil
   and simmer for about 15 minutes. If the pears are ripe, then the
   cooking time should be reduced. Allow the pears to cool standing in the wine stock.
3. Remove the pears from the pans, slice and arrange on 4 plates.
   Garnish with orange segments, orange zest and hazelnuts.
   Flood the plates with the red wine cooking liquid and serve.

MARKWICK'S
Bristol

Banana Curry Soup
Fish Stew with Leeks and Saffron
Pears Poached in Marsala with Sabayon Sauce

Serves 4–6

Banana Curry Soup

25 g (1 oz) butter
1 small onion, skinned and
  chopped
2.5 ml (½ tsp) curry powder
900 ml (1½ pints) light
  chicken stock

350 g (12 oz) ripe bananas,
  peeled and chopped
30 ml (2 tbsp) lemon juice
salt
150 ml (¼ pint) single
  cream

1. Melt the butter in a pan and sweat the onion for 5 minutes. Stir in
   the curry powder and cook for a further 30 seconds or so.
2. Add the stock, bananas, lemon juice and salt to taste. Bring to
   the boil, cover and simmer gently for 15 minutes.
3. Purée the soup in a blender and stir in the cream. Taste and
   adjust seasoning. Return the soup to the pan and reheat to serve.

Fish Stew with Leeks and Saffron

2 medium leeks, washed,
  cleaned and finely
  chopped
4 shallots, skinned and
  finely chopped
25 g (1 oz) butter
150 ml (¼ pint) dry white
  wine
150 ml (¼ pint) fish stock

large pinch of saffron
  strands, soaked in a little
  fish stock for about 1 hour
75 ml (3 fl oz) double cream
salt and pepper
lemon juice to taste
450–700 g (1–1½ lb)
  assorted filleted fish, such
  as cod, plaice, salmon,
  monkfish

1. Sweat the leeks and shallots in the butter until soft.
2. Place the wine and fish stock in a separate pan and reduce by half. Add the reduced liquid to the leeks, then add the soaked saffron.
3. Bring to the boil, add the cream, seasoning and lemon juice. Boil for 1 minute or so to thicken the sauce a little. Remove from the heat.
4. Meanwhile, season the fish fillets and steam gently, beginning with the monkfish if you are using this as it will take slightly longer to cook.
5. Pour the sauce into 4 shallow bowls, top with the fish and serve.

Pears Poached in Marsala with Sabayon Sauce

4 large pears, peeled
2 egg yolks
squeeze of lemon juice
toasted, slivered almonds, to decorate

Syrup:
450 g (1 lb) sugar
300 ml (½ pint) marsala
vanilla pod
lemon peel

1. For the syrup, put 600 ml (1 pint) water, the sugar, marsala, vanilla pod and lemon peel into a pan. Heat gently to dissolve the sugar, then gently simmer for 10 minutes.
2. Place the pears in the marsala flavoured sugar syrup, bring to the boil, then reduce the heat and simmer until the pears are just cooked, but not too soft. Remove them from the syrup and set aside.
3. In a bowl placed over a pan of boiling water, place the egg yolks, lemon juice and 75–100 ml (3–4 fl oz) of the poaching liquid. Whisk vigorously and continuously until the mixture is thick and frothy. Taste the sauce to see if the egg yolks have been cooked out. (It should not taste of raw egg.)
4. Place a pear in the centre of a shallow individual flameproof dish and pour over the sabayon. Place the dish under a hot grill to brown if required. Garnish with toasted almonds.

THE MARSH GOOSE
Moreton in Marsh, Gloucestershire

Salmon Strudel
Venison Casserole with Shallots and Thyme
Hot Apricot Pudding

Serves 4–6

Salmon Strudel

Strudel paste:
225 g (8 oz) soft flour
pinch of salt
1 egg
1 egg yolk
90 ml (3½ fl oz) warm milk
25 g (1 oz) melted butter

Salmon mousse:
450 g (1 lb) salmon, minced and sieved
1 egg white
10 ml (2 tsp) salt
900 ml (1½ pints) double cream
225 g (8 oz) salmon, diced

1. For the strudel paste, put the flour and salt into a mixing bowl and make a well in the centre. Add all the wet ingredients and mix by hand until it forms a smooth ball. Put into the refrigerator to rest for at least 1 hour.
2. For the salmon mousse, put the minced salmon in a food processor and mix for 30 seconds. Add the egg white and mix for a further 30 seconds. Leave to rest for at least 30 minutes in the refrigerator.
3. Put the salmon and salt into a mixing bowl and gradually beat in the double cream, stopping frequently to scrape the sides of the bowl down. When all the cream has been incorporated, leave again for at least 30 minutes before using.
4. Roll out half the strudel paste to about 30×15 cm (12×6 inches). Transfer to a floured tea towel and continue rolling and stretching, taking care not to rip the pastry, until it is about 45×30 cm (18×12 inches). (You should be able to read the *Financial Times* through the dough!)

5. Using a knife, spread the salmon mixture evenly over the paste. Then distribute the diced salmon on top of the mousse and liberally season with black pepper.
6. Using the tea towel, roll the strudel gently but firmly, pulling the back of the tea towel towards you. Place on a baking sheet and allow to rest for 30 minutes.
7. Before baking, brush with melted butter. Bake in the oven at 150°C (300°F) mark 2 for about 25 minutes.
8. The strudel may be served either hot or cold. If hot, make the following sauce. Reduce 600 ml (1 pint) fish stock to 90 ml (6 tbsp) liquid. Add 450 ml (¾ pint) double cream. Reboil, strain, season and add 30 ml (2 tbsp) chopped dill and 30 ml (2 tbsp) skinned, seeded and chopped tomatoes. If serving cold, accompany with hard-boiled quails' eggs and a salad of cucumber and chopped chives.

Venison Casserole with Shallots and Thyme

1 kg (2 lb) lean venison from the haunch, with no sinew or tendons
50 g (2 oz) seasoned flour
oil for frying
450 g (1 lb) shallots, skinned, with roots left intact
1 bunch of thyme, chopped
2.3 litres (4 pints) dark stock
salt and pepper
30 ml (2 tbsp) double cream

1. Coat the meat in the seasoned flour, shaking off any excess. Heat the oil in a heavy bottomed pan and brown the meat on all sides over a fierce heat.
2. Drain the venison in a colander and, using the same pan and a little oil, brown the shallots. Drain with the venison.
3. Put the meat, thyme and stock in a casserole, bring to the boil and season. Cook in the oven at 200°C (400°F) mark 6 for 1 hour. Add the shallots and cook for a further 30 minutes or until the venison is cooked.
4. Remove from the oven and take out the shallots and venison. Boil the cooking liquor over a fierce heat, removing any scum from the surface.
5. Adjust the seasoning, add the cream and pour the liquid over the meat and shallots. Serve with creamed potatoes and spring cabbage.

Hot Apricot Pudding

350 g (12 oz) caster sugar
100 g (4 oz) unsalted butter, softened
10 ml (2 tsp) vanilla essence
4 eggs, beaten
350 g (12 oz) soft flour
20 g (¾ oz) baking powder
350 g (12 oz) apricots, chopped
10 ml (2 tsp) bicarbonate of soda

Butterscotch sauce:
175 g (6 oz) soft dark brown sugar
100 g (4 oz) caster sugar
100 g (4 oz) unsalted butter
275 g (10 oz) golden syrup
300 ml (½ pint) double cream

1. Cream the sugar, butter and vanilla essence in a mixer for 8 minutes. Gently add the beaten eggs until thoroughly incorporated. Then fold in the flour and baking powder.
2. Bring 600 ml (1 pint) water to the boil, add the chopped apricots and boil for 2 minutes. Remove from the heat and add the bicarbonate of soda. Add to the rest of the mixture, mixing thoroughly.
3. Transfer to a buttered and floured dish measuring 30 × 15 × 7.5 cm (12 × 6 × 3 inches). Bake in the oven at 150°C (300°F) mark 2 for about 40 minutes. Test to see if ready with a skewer (it should come out clean).
4. For the sauce, bring the sugar, butter and syrup gently to the boil. Add the cream and reboil. Strain and serve hot with the apricot pudding.

LE MESURIER
London, EC1

Apple and Stilton Soup
Pork Chops with Sherry and Mushrooms
Hot Lemon Soufflé

Serves 4

Apple and Stilton Soup

60 g (2½ oz) butter
2 medium onions, skinned
and chopped
4 Golden Delicious apples,
peeled and chopped
1.1 litres (2 pints) good
home made chicken stock

90 g (3½ oz) Stilton cheese,
chopped
150 ml (¼ pint) double
cream

1. Melt the butter in a pan and cook the onions slowly until soft.
   Add the chopped apples and cook for a few more minutes.
2. Add the chicken stock, bring to the boil and cook for 5 minutes.
3. Just before serving, add the chopped Stilton cheese and cream.
   Simmer until the cheese has just melted.

Pork Chops with Sherry and Mushrooms

25 g (1 oz) butter
15 ml (1 tbsp) oil
4 pork chops, trimmed of fat
100 g (4 oz) mushrooms,
  sliced
100 ml (4 fl oz) dry sherry

300 ml (½ pint) double
  cream
salt and pepper
chopped fresh parsley,
  to garnish

1. Melt the butter and oil in an ovenproof pan and brown the pork chops on both sides. Put the lid on the frying pan and cook in the oven at 200°C (400°F) mark 6 for 8 minutes.
2. Remove the chops from the pan, reserving the juices. Place the chops on a plate in a warm oven and leave to rest until the sauce is finished.
3. Add the mushrooms to the juices left in the frying pan and cook for a few minutes. Remove with a slotted spoon and reserve with the chops.
4. Add the sherry and boil to reduce by half, then add the cream. Boil down fast until the sauce is of a coating consistency. Taste, season with salt and pepper.
5. Pour the sauce over the chops and mushrooms and sprinkle with chopped parsley.

Note: Use large flat field mushrooms if possible.

Hot Lemon Soufflé

50 g (2 oz) butter
120 g (4 oz) sugar
100 ml (6 tbsp) lemon juice,
 from about 3 lemons

4 egg yolks
grated rind of 2 lemons
5 egg whites
icing sugar for sprinkling

1. Butter the soufflé dishes really well and coat with caster sugar. Turn the dishes upside down and shake off excess sugar.
2. In a heavy based saucepan, heat the butter with half the sugar and all the lemon juice until the butter and sugar are melted. Remove from the heat.
3. Beat in the egg yolks, one by one. Add the lemon rind. Cook very gently, whisking constantly, until the mixture thickens to the consistency of double cream. Don't let it get too hot or it will separate. Keep the mixture covered at room temperature.
4. Twenty to thirty minutes before serving, heat the oven until really hot.
5. Whisk the egg whites until stiff and forming peaks. Add the remaining sugar and beat for 20 seconds longer or until glossy. Gently fold in the lemon mixture – if it looks stiff, heat gently before adding it to the whites.
6. Spoon the mixture into the prepared soufflé dishes. Flatten the tops with a knife – it must be completely level with the top of the dish. (It can now hardly fail to rise!) Wipe round the top of the dishes with a damp cloth to remove any mixture. Put into the oven on the top shelf until well risen. Sprinkle with icing sugar and serve immediately.

Note: I find that all soufflés cook best in individual soufflé dishes. In this way the soufflés remain soft in the middle and yet well risen and golden brown on top. Have the oven as hot as it will go.

MING
London, W1

Mr. Edwards' Braised Pork
Tree Mushroom Cakes
Toffee Banana/Apple

Serves 4–6

Mr. Edwards' Braised Pork

1.4 kg (3 lb) streaky pork
2 pieces Chinese cinnamon
8 cloves
Sichuan wild peppercorns
4 pieces star anise
15 ml (1 tbsp) vegetable oil
2 large spring onions,
   trimmed and cut into
   lengths

1 large piece fresh root
   ginger, peeled, coarsely
   sectioned and pounded
30 ml (2 tbsp) rice wine
22.5 ml (1½ tbsp) light soy
   sauce

1. Trim off the skin and excess fat from the pork. Cut the pork into strips or cubes, 1.5 cm (½ inch) in size.
2. Make the cinnamon, cloves, peppercorns and star anise into a spice bag.
3. Plunge the meat into boiling water for less than 1 minute. Drain and rinse in cold water. Drain well.
4. Heat the oil and sauté the spring onions and ginger until fragrant. Add the pork, rice wine and soy sauce. Stir and mix well for 2–3 minutes. Put in the sachet of spices and enough stock or water to cover the meat.
5. Bring to the boil, then turn down the heat and simmer for 1 hour. Heat gently for another 30 minutes. Taste and add salt if necessary. Serve with rice, boiled new potatoes or pasta.

Tree Mushroom Cakes

4 large pieces tree mushroom,
   select thick and open ones
225 g (8 oz) prepared squid
3 large or 4 medium prawns
2 stalks of fresh coriander
8 pieces water chestnuts
1 piece tangerine peel,
   soaked

10 ml (2 tsp) sesame oil
5 ml (1 tsp) white pepper
7.5 ml (1½ tsp) salt
37.5 ml (2½ tbsp) potato
   flour
oil for deep frying

1. Soak the tree mushroom pieces in water for at least 2 hours. Trim off the tip, which may contain dirt, then cut into small pieces.
2. Pat dry the squid and prawns on absorbent kitchen paper and cut into pieces.
3. Blend or chop all the ingredients and mix in the seasonings. Shape the cakes any size – round, long or square – by hand. Deep fry in medium hot oil until golden.
4. Serve as a starter with a slightly hot and vinegary sauce, mixed with chilli and garlic. As a one dish meal, serve with salad or stir fry vegetables.

Toffee Banana/Apple

2 large bananas, half ripe
2 large firm apples
25 g (1 oz) plain flour
25 g (1 oz) cornflour

sesame oil
90 ml (6 tbsp) white sugar
30 ml (2 tbsp) sesame seeds

1. Peel and prepare the fruits, then cut into bite size pieces, about 3 cm (1¼ inches).
2. Mix the flours in a large bowl. Add drops of oil and enough water to form a thick but pourable batter.
3. Prepare a bowl of ice water.
4. Dip the fruit pieces into the batter, using a pair of long chopsticks to drain off excess batter. Fry in hot oil (not boiling) for 2 minutes. Drain.
5. To make the toffee the easy way, heat a pan and turn down the heat to low. Spoon in the sugar; it will then melt and begin to caramelise.
6. Stir in the sesame seeds, then add the drained fruit pieces. Mix well. Dip into the ice water and serve immediately.

NEWTON'S
London, SW4

Waterfall Salad
Fish Pie with Herb and Cheese Crust
Brûléed Peaches

Serves 4

Waterfall Salad

The lime leaf, galangal and lemon grass are often available from Asian supermarkets.

1 clove of garlic, skinned
½ stalk of lemon grass
1 lime leaf (optional)
1 thin slice of galangal
½ fresh chilli
2.5 ml (½ tsp) caster sugar
juice of ½ lime

juice of ¼ lemon
225 g (8 oz) rare roast beef
**   or cooked lamb or pork**
frisée and iceberg lettuce
100 g (4 oz) rice, lightly
**   toasted under the grill**

1. Finely chop the garlic, lemon grass, lime leaf, galangal and chilli together with the sugar, lime and lemon juice.
2. Warm the roast beef in a hot pan for 10 seconds on each side. Slice the beef thinly and toss in the dressing.
3. Arrange the beef on the lettuce and top with chopped mint and toasted rice.

Fish Pie with Herb and Cheese Crust

175 g (6 oz) smoked
   haddock
175 g (6 oz) white haddock
600 ml (1 pint) milk
100 g (4 oz) prawns
   (if feeling rich)
8 cooked mussels
25 g (1 oz) butter
25 g (1 oz) plain flour
1 small glass of wine
5 ml (1 tsp) mustard

a few skinned and chopped
   tomatoes
a little caster sugar
salt and pepper
450 g (1 lb) potatoes,
   mashed
4 slices of white bread
100 g (4 oz) Cheddar
   cheese, grated
fresh chopped herbs

1. Poach the haddock fillets in the milk for 10–15 minutes. Remove the fish and flake it into an ovenproof dish. Reserve the milk. Add the prawns and the mussels.
2. Make a sauce with the butter, flour and milk from the fish. Add the wine and mustard. Pour the thick sauce over the fish.
3. Scatter the tomatoes on top, sprinkle with caster sugar, salt and pepper. Cover the pie with the mashed potatoes. Make the breadcrumbs and combine with the cheese and herbs. Spoon over the pie.
4. Bake in the oven at 200°C (400°F) mark 6 for about 15 minutes until golden.

Brûléed Peaches

4 yellow peaches
60 ml (4 tbsp) sugar
250 ml (8 fl oz) red wine
4 Amaretti biscuits

60 ml (4 tbsp) demerara
   sugar
40 ml (8 tsp) mascarpone
   cheese
4 mint leaves

1. Place the peaches in a pan and cover with 2.5 cm (1 inch) water. Add the sugar and wine and poach until cooked but firm. Allow to cool, then halve and remove the stones.
2. Crumble the Amaretti biscuits very finely and sprinkle on the cut side of the 8 peach halves. Sprinkle over the demerara sugar.
3. Place the peaches, sugar side up, on a baking sheet and grill under high heat until the sugar caramelises. Serve with mascarpone spooned into the middle and decorate with mint leaves.

NORMANDIE
Birtle, Nr Bury

Purée of Smoked Haddock
Casserole of Chicken with Pilaf Rice
Apple Strudel

Serves 4–6

Purée of Smoked Haddock

1 kg (2 lb) smoked haddock
600 ml (1 pint) olive oil
10 g (⅓ oz) garlic, skinned
  and crushed
250 ml (9 fl oz) single cream
salt and pepper
thin toast, to serve

Garnish:
lettuce leaves
fine green beans, blanched
vinaigrette

1. Soak the smoked haddock in fresh water. Change the water two to three times. Cut the fish into pieces.
2. Poach the fish gently in fresh water for 8 minutes. Strain. Remove skin and bone, then flake the fish.
3. Heat 200 ml (7 fl oz) of the olive oil until very hot. Add the haddock and garlic and mix gently until incorporated. Add the remaining olive oil and the single cream. Season well. (The mixture should be the consistency of mashed potato.)
4. Place the purée onto rounds of thin toast. Garnish with lettuce leaves and beans. Sprinkle with vinaigrette and serve immediately.

Casserole of Chicken with Pilaf Rice

1–2 kg (2–4 lb) chicken
75 g (3 oz) onion, skinned
75 g (3 oz) carrot, peeled
75 g (3 oz) leek, cleaned
25 g (1 oz) celery
10 g (⅓ oz) garlic, skinned
bouquet garni (see method)
cloves
sea salt and pepper
10 ml (2 tsp) cream

Pilaf rice:
75 g (3 oz) onion, skinned
and chopped

250 g (9 oz) rice
chicken stock
butter for cooking

Garnish:
120 g (4½ oz) button
mushrooms
120 g (4½ oz) button
onions, skinned
5 ml (1 tsp) butter
sugar
chopped fresh parsley

1. In a flameproof casserole, place the chicken and cover with fresh water. Bring to the boil and skim the surface. Prepare a bouquet garni using leek, thyme, parsley and bay leaves.
2. Add the onion, carrot, leek, celery, garlic, bouquet garni, cloves and seasoning and cook gently for 40 minutes. Remove the chicken from the stock. Strain the stock and reserve.
3. For the pilaf rice, gently cook the chopped onion in butter in a flameproof casserole. Add the rice and fry for 2–3 minutes. Add boiled chicken stock (1½ times the volume of rice). Cook in the oven at 200°C (400°F) mark 6 for 17 minutes.
4. For the garnish, seal the button mushrooms and onions in the butter with sugar and seasoning. Add 100 ml (4 fl oz) chicken stock, cover and simmer for 2 minutes until the vegetables are well glazed.
5. Reduce 1 litre (1¾ pints) chicken stock and add the cream. Bring back to the boil. Season. Sieve and keep in a warm place.
6. Bone the chicken and put on a plate, add the vegetable garnish and sauce. Serve the rice separately in a bowl. Sprinkle with chopped parsley.

Apple Strudel

4 large sheets of filo pastry
25 g (1 oz) butter, melted
25 g (1 oz) icing sugar

Sauce:
150 g (5 oz) caster sugar
100 ml (4 fl oz) water
50 ml (2 fl oz) Calvados
250 ml (8 fl oz) double
  cream

Filling:
100 g (4 oz) raisins

splash of rum and brandy
grated zest of ½ orange
700 g (1½ lb) cooking
  apples, peeled, cored and
  diced
50 g (2 oz) butter
100 g (4 oz) sugar
15 ml (1 tbsp) honey
large pinch of ground
  cinnamon
50–75 g (2–3 oz) fresh
  breadcrumbs

1. For the sauce, put the sugar and water in a pan and heat until golden and caramelised. Add the Calvados to the caramel, taking care as it bubbles. Boil gently until the alcohol evaporates and add the cream. Bring back to the boil and set aside.
2. For the filling, soak the raisins with rum and brandy and add the orange zest.
3. Sauté the apples in the butter, sugar, honey and cinnamon until caramelised but still firm. Leave to cool.
4. Butter each sheet of filo and dust with icing sugar. Stack the sheets on top of each other.
5. Spread the breadcrumbs in the middle of the pastry and place the apple and raisins on top. Leave the edges free. Roll the strudel and put on a buttered tray. Bake in the oven at 220°C (425°F) mark 7 for about 15 minutes.
6. Pour some sauce on each plate with a slice of strudel and serve.

ODETTE'S
London, NW1

Spicy Crab Minestrone
Home Smoked Pigeon Breasts, Pancetta and Lentils
Pavlova with Fudge Sauce

Serves 4–6

Spicy Crab Minestrone

1 kg (2¼ lb) green crabs
100 g (4 oz) smoked bacon, chopped
1 large onion, skinned and chopped
2 carrots, peeled and chopped
½ bulb of garlic, skinned and crushed
1 red pepper, seeded
100 ml (4 fl oz) brandy
¼ bottle white wine
2.3 litres (4 pints) fish stock
100 ml (4 fl oz) tomato juice
pinch of saffron
1 chilli, chopped
salt and pepper
10 ml (2 tsp) harissa paste
olive oil
thin slices of courgette, carrot and leek, to serve
chopped fresh parsley, to garnish

1. Sauté the crabs and smoked bacon in a large pan with the onion, carrots and garlic.
2. Chargrill the red pepper. Skin, core, seed, chop and add to the mixture. Flame the mixture with brandy; extinguish with the wine. Add the fish stock, tomato juice, saffron and chilli.
3. Season and add the harissa paste and some olive oil. Cover and cook in the oven at 170°C (325°F) mark 3 for about 2 hours.
4. Strain out all the shells, feathery crab gills and vegetables. Correct the seasoning. Serve with thin slices of courgette, carrot and leeks. Garnish with chopped parsley.

Home Smoked Pigeon Breasts, Pancetta and Lentils

6 pigeon breasts (one per
  portion)
450 g (1 lb) Puy lentils,
  soaked overnight
4 sprigs of rosemary
1 bulb of garlic, skinned
salt
6 slices of pancetta
30 ml (2 tbsp) red wine
1.1 litres (2 pints) pigeon or
  game stock

To smoke pigeons:
one 5–7.5 cm (2–3 inch)
  deep tray
wood shavings
wire rack
foil

1. To smoke the pigeon breasts, cover the bottom of the deep tray with about 1 cm (½ inch) wood shavings. Lay a wire rack on top, making sure it does not touch the shavings. Place the pigeon breasts on the rack, breast down, and cover with foil. Place carefully over a naked flame until the shavings are smoking. Leave for about 3–4 minutes. Remove from the heat and leave to cool down.
2. Drain and cover the lentils with water. Add the rosemary and garlic. Simmer until soft. Add salt, then drain.
3. Fry the sliced pancetta until crisp. Add the lentils and season.
4. Seal the smoked pigeon breasts in a hot frying pan. Place in the oven at 220°C (425°F) mark 7 and cook until pink, about 8–10 minutes. Set aside the pigeon breasts. Deglaze the pan with red wine, reduce, add the stock and simmer to taste.
5. Arrange the lentils and pancetta on plates. Place a pigeon breast on top and finally add the sauce.

Pavlova with Fudge Sauce

6 egg whites, size 1 or 2
200 g (7 oz) caster sugar
30 ml (2 tbsp) potato flour
15 ml (1 tbsp) white wine
  vinegar
whipped cream and
  seasonal fruit, to serve

Fudge sauce (optional):
250 g (9 oz) caster sugar
250 ml (8 fl oz) double
  cream

1. Whisk the egg whites to soft peak stage. Gradually whisk in the sugar until the meringue is very stiff and glossy. Beat in the potato flour and vinegar thoroughly.
2. Pile the meringue evenly into a well greased and lined 23 cm (9 inch) springform pan. Bake in the oven at 150°C (300°F) mark 2 for about 25 minutes until well risen, pale golden and deeply cracked.
3. Cool in the tin for 30 minutes, then unclip the tin. Serve with softly whipped cream and seasonal fruit or fudge sauce.
4. For the fudge sauce, melt the caster sugar in a heavy pan over a medium heat until deep golden brown. Add the double cream, standing well back to avoid the spitting caramel. Stir over a low heat until fully dissolved.

BISTRO 190
London, SW7

Tomato Bisque
Mediterranean Sandwich
Tropical Fruit Pavlova

Serves 4–6

Tomato Bisque

2 slices white bread, crusts removed
15 ml (1 tbsp) red wine vinegar
3 cloves of garlic, skinned
15 ml (1 tbsp) caster sugar
75 ml (3 fl oz) extra virgin olive oil
700 g (1½ lb) tomatoes, skinned and sliced
900 ml (1½ pints) tomato juice

4 spring onions, trimmed and sliced
½ cucumber, peeled and roughly sliced
1 red pepper, roasted, peeled and seeded
1 red chilli, roasted and peeled
10 fresh basil leaves, finely chopped

1. Crumble the bread in a food processor. Add the vinegar and blend, then the garlic and caster sugar.
2. With the processor running, add as much olive oil as the bread will absorb without becoming oily.
3. Add all the remaining ingredients and blend until smooth.

Mediterranean Sandwich

1 large country loaf
1 clove of garlic, skinned
75 ml (3 fl oz) extra virgin olive oil
60 ml (4 tbsp) tapenade
30 large basil leaves
8 roasted tomato halves
60 ml (4 tbsp) pesto
150 g (5 oz) aubergine slices, grilled
four 100 g (4 oz) buffalo mozzarella, sliced
115 g (4½ oz) yellow pepper, roasted, peeled and quartered

115 g (4½ oz) black olives, stoned
50 g (2 oz) red onion, skinned and diced
50 g (2 oz) rocket leaves
15 ml (1 tbsp) balsamic vinegar
150 g (5 oz) courgette slices, grilled
150 g (5 oz) sun-dried tomatoes
115 g (4½ oz) red pepper, roasted, peeled and quartered
50 g (2 oz) baby spinach

1. Cut 2.5 cm (1 inch) off the top of the country loaf; hollow out the soft bread leaving 2 cm (¾ inch) all round.
2. Rub the bread with garlic and dribble with olive oil. Spread thinly with a layer of tapenade.
3. Next, place the basil leaves, then the tomato halves, pesto, aubergine slices, mozzarella, yellow pepper, black olives, red onion, rocket leaves, balsamic vinegar, courgette slices, sun-dried tomatoes, mozzarella, red pepper and baby spinach into the bar. Pepper each layer lightly.
4. Replace the bread lid. Wrap the whole loaf in cling film and place under a heavy weight, preferably overnight.
5. Cut in wedges and serve with a warm potato salad and rock salt.

Tropical Fruit Pavlova

4 egg whites
2.5 ml (½ tsp) salt
225 g (8 oz) caster sugar
20 ml (4 tsp) cornflour
2.5 ml (½ tsp) vanilla
  essence
7.5 ml (1½ tsp) white wine
  vinegar

12 baby kiwi fruits
1 mango
½ pineapple
2 bananas
12 lychees
6 rambutan
150 ml (¼ pint) double
  cream

1. Whisk the egg whites with the salt until stiff. Whisk in the sugar, little by little, then whisk until the mixture is glossy and very stiff. Fold in the cornflour, vanilla and vinegar.
2. Spoon the mixture onto a 23 cm (9 inch) circle drawn on baking parchment. Make the sides higher than the middle so that the centre becomes an open basket.
3. Bake in the oven at 140°C (275°F) mark 1 for about 1½ hours; turn off the oven and allow to cool.
4. Prepare all the fruit and cut into pieces. Whip the cream until fairly stiff and fold in some of the fruits leaving the remainder for decoration. Fill the pavlova shell with the mixture.

192
London, W11

Beetroot and Celeriac Soup
Country Sausage Stew
Filo of Apples, Pears and Orange Sabayon

Serves 4–6

Beetroot and Celeriac Soup

30 ml (2 tbsp) olive oil
4 beetroot, peeled and
  roughly chopped
1 celeriac, peeled and
  roughly chopped
2 potatoes, peeled and
  roughly chopped
1 onion, skinned and
  roughly chopped
1 chilli, seeded and finely
  chopped

7.5 ml (1½ tsp) ground
  cumin
2 good pinches of oregano
5 cloves of garlic, skinned
finely grated rind and juice
  of 1 orange
salt and pepper
dash of white wine vinegar

1. Warm the oil in a large soup pot and add the beetroot, celeriac,
   potatoes, onion, chilli, cumin, oregano and garlic. Lightly sauté
   for 5 minutes.
2. Cover with 600 ml (1 pint) water and simmer for 1 hour. Remove
   from the heat when the beetroot and celeriac are soft, and add
   the orange rind and juice.
3. To finish the soup, purée in a blender, then add salt and pepper
   to taste. Also add a dash of white wine vinegar to bring out the
   taste.

Country Sausage Stew

oil for cooking
700 g (1½ lb) pork sausages
550 g (1¼ lb) spicy sausages
3 onions, skinned and cubed
1 green pepper, seeded and
  cubed
1 red pepper, seeded and
  cubed
4 cloves of garlic, skinned
1 chicken stock cube,
  dissolved in 100 ml
  (4 fl oz) hot water
100 ml (4 fl oz) white wine
3 potatoes, peeled and
  cubed
1 can tomatoes
30 ml (2 tbsp) tomato paste
pinch of oregano, basil and
  thyme
1 pack frozen green beans
¼ savoy cabbage, roughly
  chopped
Parmesan cheese and
  croûtons, to garnish

1. Heat a heavy based saucepan with a dash of oil. Add the
   sausages and cook until brown, turning occasionally. Remove
   the sausages from the pan and cut into 5 cm (2 inch) pieces.
2. Add the onions, peppers and garlic and sauté until the peppers
   and onion are soft. Pour in the stock and wine, adding the potatoes, tomatoes, tomato paste and herbs. Continue to cook until
   the potatoes soften.
3. Return the sausages to the pan, adding the green beans and cabbage, and cook for a further 10 minutes. Serve garnished with
   Parmesan and croûtons.

Filo of Apples, Pears and Orange Sabayon

1 packet filo pastry
sunflower oil for brushing

Filling:
2 apples, peeled and cored
2 pears, peeled and cored
juice of ½ lemon
1 bunch of mint, chopped
15 ml (1 tbsp) caster sugar
pinch of ground cinnamon

Sabayon:
5 egg yolks
10 g (⅓ oz) caster sugar
3 oranges (juice of all, zest
  of one)
30 ml (2 tbsp) brandy,
  preferably Calvados
icing sugar for dusting

1. Filo pastry is sometimes difficult as it dries out quickly and needs to be dealt with rapidly. Lay 2 filo sheets out flat and cut out rounds 15 cm (6 inches) in diameter. Repeat cutting out the rounds; 3 double thickness rounds per person. Cover with a lightly dampened cloth; remove the rounds from the cloth as required.

2. Lightly brush the filo with sunflower oil and cook in the oven at 180°C (350°F) mark 4 until golden. Remove and allow to cool on a wire rack.

3. For the filling, chop the apples and pears quite small. Coat with the lemon juice, chopped mint, sugar and cinnamon straight away. Leave to stand at room temperature.

4. For the sabayon, beat the egg yolks, sugar, orange juice and zest over a double boiler until the mixture thickens. Add the brandy, whisk again and keep warm.

5. To serve, place one filo round on a plate with some of the filling and a spoonful of sabayon on top, finely spread to within 2.5 cm (1 inch) of the edge. Place another round on top and repeat, topping with a third round of filo. Sprinkle a little icing sugar on top and serve.

OSTERIA ANTICA BOLOGNA
London, SW11

Clam and Courgette Soup
Pasta with Spinach and Sun-Dried Tomatoes
Tiramisu

Serves 4–6

Clam and Courgette Soup

450 g (1 lb) fresh baby
  clams in their shells
6 medium courgettes
1 medium onion, skinned
  and finely chopped
1 large potato, peeled and
  diced

60 ml (4 tbsp) olive oil
salt and pepper
2 cloves of garlic, skinned
  and chopped
3 basil leaves, chopped
1 handful of parsley,
  chopped

1. Stand the clams in a large bowl of cold salty water for 3–4 hours to remove the grit.
2. Chop 4 of the courgettes finely. Lightly sauté the chopped courgettes with the onion and potato in 30 ml (2 tbsp) of the olive oil for about 5 minutes until the onions are transparent. Add salt and pepper to taste, then add 2 litres (3½ pints) water. Bring to the boil, reduce the heat and simmer for 20 minutes. Leave to cool slightly, then liquidize or sieve the soup.
3. Meanwhile, put the cleaned clams in a very large pan with the garlic and remaining olive oil. Put the pan over a medium heat and cover. Shake the pan over the heat for about 9 minutes until the clams open. Any that have not opened by this time should be thrown away. Add the juices used to cook the clams to the soup.
4. Slice the remaining 2 courgettes into thin short lengths. Add to the soup with the basil and parsley. Bring the soup back to the boil, simmer for 5 minutes, then add the clams. Serve with a drizzle of olive oil over the soup.

Pasta with Spinach and Sun-dried Tomatoes

450 g (1 lb) spinach
salt and pepper
500 g (1 lb 2 oz)
   Strozzapreti pasta
10 sun-dried tomatoes in
   oil, finely chopped

45 ml (3 tbsp) olive oil
2 cloves of garlic
3 fresh chillies, finely
   chopped
200 g (7 oz) stoned black
   olives

1. Carefully wash the spinach two or three times in a bowl with lots of cold water. Rinse well, so that any dirt remains in the bowl, not on the spinach. When washed, chop roughly into strips and leave to one side.
2. Bring 4.5 litres (1 gallon) of salted water to the boil. Add the pasta and cook for about 10 minutes until 'al dente'.
3. Meanwhile, sauté the tomatoes in the olive oil with the garlic and chillies for 2 minutes. Then add the olives and spinach. Toss over a moderate heat, coating with the olive oil mixture.
4. Finally add the drained pasta and toss over moderate heat to amalgamate all the ingredients. Serve immediately.

Tiramisu

3 eggs, separated
60 ml (4 tbsp) icing sugar,
   sifted
45 ml (3 tbsp) brandy
30 ml (2 tbsp) amaretto
   liqueur
400 g (14 oz) mascarpone
   cheese

1 large packet of savoiardi
   biscuits
about 600 ml (1 pint)
   freshly made espresso
   coffee
100 g (4 oz) bitter chocolate,
   pulverized in a blender

1. Whisk the egg whites and put to one side. Beat the egg yolks together, then add the icing sugar, brandy and amaretto and beat until the mixture is smooth. Once smooth, beat in the mascarpone cheese. Finally fold in the beaten egg whites.
2. Cover the bottom of a large baking tray with a thin layer of this mixture. Dip the savoiardi biscuits in the espresso coffee and layer them over the mixture, completely covering the tray. Follow with another layer of the mascarpone mixture, then a fourth of savoiardi dipped in espresso coffee.
3. Finish with a layer of mascarpone cream on top and sprinkle the chocolate over this final layer. Chill for 2–3 hours before serving.

POMEGRANATES
London, SW1

Lamb Meatballs with Quails' Eggs
Pang Pang Chicken
Honey and Cognac Ice Cream

Serves 4

Lamb Meatballs with Quails' Eggs

550 g (1¼ lb) minced lamb
2.5 cm (1 inch) piece of fresh root ginger, peeled and chopped
2.5 ml (½ tsp) chilli powder
5 ml (1 tsp) ground cumin
15 ml (1 tbsp) ground coriander
1 onion, skinned and finely chopped

2 cloves of garlic, skinned and crushed
40 g (1½ oz) gram chick-pea flour
5 ml (1 tsp) salt
2.5 ml (½ tsp) black pepper
1 egg
12 hard-boiled quails' eggs
vegetable oil for deep-frying

1. Combine all the ingredients, except the quails' eggs and oil, together until they are well blended. Divide the mixture into twelve equal portions. Using damp hands, roll each portion into a ball, then flatten with the palm of your hand.
2. Put a hard-boiled quail egg in the centre of the meat. Bring the meat up and around it to enclose completely. Put the balls in a greased dish and chill in the refrigerator for 30 minutes.
3. Fill a large deep frying pan one third full with oil and heat until hot. Carefully lower the meatballs into the oil, a few at a time, and fry for 2–3 minutes or until crisp and golden brown. Transfer to absorbent kitchen paper to drain.
4. To serve, allow 3 meatballs per person, skewered on bamboo sticks. Accompany with tomato and apple chutney, yogurt and cucumber raita and rice.

Pang Pang Chicken

275 g (10 oz) cucumber, peeled
5 ml (1 tsp) salt
600 ml (1 pint) clear stock or water
2 chicken breasts, 450 g (1 lb) boned
8 spring onions, white parts only, trimmed and cut into silken threads

Dressing:
20 ml (4 tsp) sesame paste or tahini
30 ml (2 tbsp) thin soy sauce
5 ml (1 tsp) rice or white wine vinegar
7.5 ml (1½ tsp) sugar
20 ml (4 tsp) hot chilli oil
2.5 ml (½ tsp) roasted Szechwan peppercorns
5 ml (1 tsp) sesame oil

1. Halve the cucumber lengthways and scoop out the seedy pulp from the centre. Cut the cucumber into thin slices. Sprinkle the salt over the cucumber and mix well. Set aside to exude the water.
2. Put the stock in a saucepan and bring to the boil. Add the chicken and poach for about 15 minutes or until cooked. Remove the chicken breasts and leave to cool.
3. For the dressing, stir the sesame paste in a jar. Add the soy sauce, vinegar, sugar, oil, peppercorns and sesame oil.
4. Rinse the cucumber in cold water to rid it of the salt, then squeeze out excess water. Arrange attractively on a serving plate.
5. When the chicken breasts are cool enough to handle, beat lightly on the skin side with a wooden spoon to loosen the fibres. Peel off the skin and tear the meat into long strips with your fingers. Arrange them in the centre of the plate. Place the spring onions on top of the chicken.
6. When ready to eat, pour the well stirred dressing over the ingredients and mix to coat. Serve cold.

Note: This dish can be prepared hours in advance and refrigerated, covered, until ready to serve. It keeps quite well until the following day, although the dressing inevitably becomes a little watery.

Honey and Cognac Ice Cream

6 eggs
225 g (8 oz) icing sugar,
  sifted
225 g (8 oz) clear honey

Cognac – enough to fill the
  empty honey jar
425 ml (15 fl oz) double
  cream

1. Separate the eggs into different bowls. Whisk the whites until stiff. Add the icing sugar and whisk until very white and stiff.
2. In another bowl, beat the egg yolks. Combine with the honey and the Cognac. Add to the egg white mixture and blend.
3. Mix in the cream and blend together. Freeze for 2–3 hours. Serve with langue de chat biscuits.

RANSOME'S DOCK
London, SW11

Pasta with Sun-dried Tomatoes, Basil and Pine Kernels
Casserole of Pheasant, Duck and Toulouse Sausage
Ransome's Dock Treacle Tart

Serves 4–6

Pasta with Sun-dried Tomatoes, Basil and Pine Kernels

500–750 g (1–1½ lb) dried
  or fresh shell pasta
one 250 g (9 oz) jar
  sun-dried tomatoes in
  olive oil, shredded
salt and pepper

2 bunches of fresh basil, cut
  in very thin strips
freshly grated Parmesan
30 ml (2 tbsp) toasted pine
  kernels, salted

1. Cook the pasta in boiling salted water, according to directions
   on the packet. Drain and keep hot.
2. In a separate pan, gently heat some of the oil from the sun-dried
   tomatoes. Add the tomatoes, pepper, basil, then the pasta, salt
   and a little Parmesan. Warm all through for 1 minute, stirring
   thoroughly.
3. Serve in a bowl and sprinkle with the pine kernels. Add extra
   Parmesan to taste.

Casserole of Pheasant, Duck and Toulouse Sausage

This casserole can be made with both the pheasant and duck, or only one if you prefer. It is essentially a variation on the cassoulet theme.

2 carrots, peeled
2 leeks, washed
2 turnips, peeled
2 parsnips, peeled
15 ml (1 tbsp) butter
small bunch of fresh thyme
3 bay leaves
2 cloves of garlic, skinned and crushed
1 whole pheasant, jointed
4 duck legs or 2 duck breasts
450 g (1 lb) Toulouse sausage or similar (Cumberland)

oil for cooking
15 ml (1 tbsp) tomato purée
600 ml (1 pint) robust red wine
600 ml (1 pint) very hot stock or water
salt and pepper
450 g (1 lb) dry butter beans (organic if possible), soaked overnight in cold water

1. Cut the vegetables into 1 cm (½ inch) cubes. In a large saucepan or casserole, brown all the vegetables in the butter. Add the herbs and garlic.
2. Seal the meat and sausages in hot oil in a frying pan. Add to the vegetables with the tomato purée.
3. Turn up the heat, add the red wine by degrees, then the stock or water, and finally the drained butter beans. Add pepper to taste, but wait until the dish is nearly cooked before adding salt.
4. Bring to a simmer, cover and cook gently for about 1 hour or until the butter beans are soft (they will absorb lots of the liquid during the cooking).
5. This dish has everything in it, and needs no other vegetables to accompany. When ready, serve with some warm fresh bread, a salad and a bottle of good red Rhône or Australian Shiraz.

Ransome's Dock Treacle Tart

Pastry:
175 g (6 oz) butter
225 g (8 oz) plain flour
1 egg

Filling:
grated rind and juice of
   2 lemons
75–90 ml (5–6 tbsp) golden
   syrup
5 ml (1 tsp) black treacle
100 g (4 oz) fresh
   wholemeal bread

1. To make the pastry, rub the butter into the flour in a bowl. Mix in the egg and knead gently. Leave the pastry to rest for 1 hour.
2. Line a large deep metal tart tin with the pastry. Bake blind in the oven at 200°C (400°F) mark 6 for 5–10 minutes or until light golden brown.
3. Put the bread into a food processor and make fine crumbs. Add the lemon rind, juice, syrup and treacle. Spoon the mixture into the pastry case.
4. Lower the oven temperature to 180°C (350°F) mark 4 and bake for about 35 minutes.

THE RED FORT
London, W1

Chilli Fish Cakes
Spiced Lamb
Vegetable Korma
Cumin Fried Basmati Rice
Ground Rice Pudding

Serves 4–6

Chilli Fish Cakes

**350 g (12 oz) fresh cod
   fillet**
¼ lime
2 potatoes, peeled
oil for cooking
**2 onions, skinned and finely
   chopped**

**2 green chillies, finely
   chopped**
**25–50 ml (1–2 fl oz) thin
   batter**
dash of bicarbonate of soda
salt to taste

1. Steam the fish with the lime squeezed over, then finely flake it.
   Boil the potatoes and mash them.
2. Heat a little oil in a pan and add the onions and green chillies.
   Add the potatoes and fish and sauté all the ingredients, mixing
   well. Shape the mixture into small cakes.
3. Make a thin batter and add bicarbonate of soda and salt. Dip the
   fish cakes in the batter and gently fry. Garnish with iceberg lettuce, tomato and cucumber, and serve with a tomato chutney.

Spiced Lamb

450 g (1 lb) lamb, cubed
225 ml (7 fl oz) thick
  natural yogurt or curd
3 onions, skinned
3 green chillies
3 dried red chillies
handful of fresh coriander
  leaves
1 clove of garlic, skinned and
  crushed
1 cm (½ inch) fresh root
  ginger, peeled and chopped

15 g (½ oz) poppy seeds
5 ml (1 tsp) ground
  coriander
25 g (1 oz) desiccated
  coconut
30 ml (2 tbsp) cooking oil
salt to taste
2.5 ml (½ tsp) garam masala

1. Soak the meat in the yogurt or curd for 30 minutes.
2. Grind together half the onion, the green chillies, red chillies, coriander leaves, garlic, ginger, poppy seeds, ground coriander and coconut. Slice the remaining onion.
3. Heat some oil in a pan and fry the onion gently. Add the ground spices and fry for a couple of minutes. Add the meat and curd with some salt.
4. Simmer until the lamb is tender, adding water if required. When cooked, sprinkle garam masala on top.

Vegetable Korma

100 g (4 oz) carrots, peeled
100 g (4 oz) fine beans
100 g (4 oz) green pepper,
  seeded
100 g (4 oz) red pepper,
  seeded
100 g (4 oz) peas
100 g (4 oz) sweetcorn
100 g (4 oz) cauliflower
225 g (8 oz) tomatoes,
  skinned

2 onions, skinned
15 ml (1 tbsp) cooking oil
1 clove of garlic, skinned
small piece of fresh root
  ginger
5 ml (1 tsp) chilli powder
5 ml (1 tsp) ground
  turmeric
salt to taste
fresh coriander leaves, to
  garnish

1. Dice all the vegetables. Cook the vegetables, except the tomatoes and onions, in boiling salted water, then set aside.
2. Purée the onion to a paste with a little water in a blender. Heat the oil in a pan and sauté the onion paste. Blend the garlic and ginger into a paste, add to the onion and fry for a few minutes. Add the chilli powder, turmeric and tomatoes, cooking for a few more minutes.
3. Add all the vegetables and salt. Simmer until the oil rises to the top. Garnish with coriander leaves

Cumin Fried Basmati Rice

450 g (1 lb) Basmati rice
butter

5 ml (1 tsp) cumin seeds
salt

1. Wash the rice thoroughly and drain. When dry, melt a knob of butter in a pan and cook the rice and cumin seeds over a gentle heat for a few minutes until the grains begin to glisten.
2. Add 900 ml (1½ pints) boiling salted water, increase the heat and bring to the boil. When the water reduces to the rice level, place a lid on the pan and reduce the heat to minimum for a further 10 minutes. Turn off and wait for a further 5 minutes.

Ground Rice Pudding

500 ml (17 fl oz) milk
100 g (4 oz) rice flour
250 g (9 oz) sugar
5 ml (1 tsp) black cardamom
** seeds**

15 ml (1 tbsp) raisins
2 blanched almonds, sliced
5 ml (1 tsp) rosewater
12 pistachio nuts, to
** decorate**

1. Bring the milk to the boil in a large saucepan. Meanwhile, mix the rice flour with 150 ml (¼ pint) water. Add to the boiling milk, stir and simmer for 10 minutes.
2. Add the sugar, cardamom seeds and raisins, then the almonds and rosewater. Keep simmering and stirring until the mixture is thick and creamy. Spoon the pudding into individual bowls and decorate with pistachios. Serve chilled.

RESTAURANT AND ARTS BAR
London, W1

Apple and Celeriac Soup
Arts Pigeon with Savoy Cabbage
Fried Bananas with Papaya and Calvados

Serves 4–6

Apple and Celeriac Soup

2 large onions, skinned and
   finely diced
25 g (1 oz) butter
4 small celeriac, peeled and
   chopped
1 stick of celery, chopped
1 leek, washed and chopped
1 potato, peeled and
   chopped
4 apples, peeled, cored and
   diced
salt and pepper
cream, to serve

1. Sweat the onions in the butter until transparent. Add the remaining vegetables and apples. Pour in 1.1 litres (2 pints) water, bring to the boil and cook for about 15 minutes.
2. When the vegetables are soft, purée the soup in a blender. Season and add cream.

Arts Pigeon with Savoy Cabbage

6 pigeons
olive oil
1 onion, skinned and
   chopped
1 carrot, peeled and
   chopped
1 clove of garlic, skinned
   and crushed
sprig of thyme
2 savoy cabbages
1 punnet of cranberries
15 ml (1 tbsp) port

1. Remove the breasts from the pigeons; soak in olive oil and put aside.
2. Chop the carcasses and brown in the oven at 200°C (400°F) mark 6 for 20 minutes. Add the onion, carrot, garlic and sprig of thyme. Cook for 10 minutes, then drain away the fat. Add 1.1 litres (2 pints) water, bring to the boil and simmer for 1 hour.
3. Remove the outside leaves from the savoy cabbages. Blanch 10 leaves, then dry on a cloth. Chop the remaining cabbage and blanch.
4. Line a casserole with the 10 cabbage leaves; lay the chopped cabbage, pigeon breasts and cranberries in layers.
5. Reduce the strained stock by half and add the port. Pour over the casserole. Poach for about 20 minutes or until the pigeon breasts are cooked. Turn out onto a plate and pour the sauce over.

Fried Bananas with Papaya and Calvados

6 medium bananas, peeled
cornflour
150 ml (¼ pint) vegetable oil
50 g (2 oz) butter

50 g (2 oz) sugar
2 papaya, sliced
25 ml (5 tsp) Calvados
icing sugar for dusting

1. Cut the bananas into quarter pieces, then coat in cornflour. Deep fry in oil. Drain and keep warm.
2. Melt the butter in a pan and add the sugar. Cook for a few seconds until caramelised. Mix in the papaya slices and Calvados.
3. Pour the mixture over the warm bananas and dust with icing sugar. In addition, or alternatively, serve with a spoonful of natural yogurt.

RIVA
London, SW13

Grilled Seasonal Vegetables
Casserole of Lamb Shanks and Lager
Boiled Cream Pudding (panna cotta)

Serves 4–6

Grilled Seasonal Vegetables

2 large red peppers	100 g (4 oz) chanterelles
2 large yellow peppers	salt
2 large courgettes	1 fresh chilli
1 large aubergine	sprig of mint
2 heads of radicchio	extra virgin olive oil

1. Blacken the skins of the peppers under the grill. Leave them to cool, then peel, halve and remove the stalks and seeds.
2. Slice the courgettes in half lengthways, slice the aubergine into 6. Cut the radicchio lengthways into 6. Place all the vegetables on absorbent kitchen paper, sprinkle with salt and leave for 30 minutes.
3. Using a very hot griddle, cook all the vegetables for about 2 minutes on each side.
4. Arrange on a plate, sprinkle with a little chopped fresh chilli, mint leaves and olive oil.

Casserole of Lamb Shanks and Lager

4 small lamb shanks
50 g (2 oz) Dijon mustard
salt and pepper
olive oil
rosemary
sage leaves
½ large onion, skinned and
  chopped

2 glasses of white wine
300 ml (½ pint) lager
600 ml (1 pint) chicken
  stock
25 g (1 oz) flour
50 g (2 oz) butter

1. Cover the lamb shanks with the mustard. Season and lightly brown in olive oil in a baking dish over the heat together with the rosemary, sage and onion.
2. Pour the wine over and cover with foil. Cook in the oven at 180°C (350°F) mark 4 for about 1½ hours or until the lamb is cooked, adding lager and stock at intervals during cooking.
3. Blend the flour and butter together. Add in pieces to the casserole to thicken. Serve the lamb with mashed potatoes or polenta.

Boiled Cream Pudding (panna cotta)

600 ml (1 pint) double
  cream
150 g (5 oz) caster sugar
vanilla essence

lemon rind
small glass of Amaretto
3 leaves of gelatine

1. Heat the cream with the sugar, vanilla and lemon rind over medium heat. Soften the gelatine in a little cold water.
2. When the cream reaches boiling point, remove from the heat and remove the lemon rind. Add the gelatine to the pan with the Amaretto, mixing well with a wooden spoon. Pour the mixture into a mould and leave to set.

LA RIVE GAUCHE
London, SE1

Marinated Chicken on Beansprout Salad
Fillet of Lamb with Vegetable Spaghetti
Bavarois with Ginger Caramel

Serves 4

Marinated Chicken on a Beansprout Salad

2 small boneless, skinless chicken breasts, cut in fine slivers
lemon juice
soy sauce
clear honey
salt and pepper

100 g (4 oz) beansprouts
50 g (2 oz) cucumber, cut into julienne strips
2 spring onions, trimmed and sliced
15 g (½ oz) fresh root ginger, finely chopped

1. Marinate the chicken in lemon juice, soy sauce, clear honey and salt and pepper.
2. Mix the beansprouts, cucumber, spring onions and ginger together. Place on a serving plate.
3. Sauté the marinated chicken in a very hot frying pan for no more than 3 minutes. Arrange on top of the salad.

Fillet of Lamb withVegetable Spaghetti

2 fillets of lamb
2 courgettes
2 carrots, peeled
¾ celeriac, peeled

butter for cooking
150 ml (¼ pint) rosemary
    flavoured gravy

1. Seal the lamb in a hot pan. Roast in the oven at 220°C (425°F) mark 7 for about 12 minutes.
2. Cut the courgettes, carrots and celeriac into long strips. Cook in a pan with a knob of butter until tender.
3. To serve, slice the lamb fillet into fine slices and arrange on top of the vegetable strips. Pour rosemary gravy around the dish.
4. Serve with gratin dauphinoise.

Bavarois with Ginger Caramel

2 leaves of gelatine
250 g (9 oz) 30% fromage
    blanc
250 ml (8 fl oz) whipped
    cream

250 g (9 oz) sugar
25 g (1 oz) candied ginger,
    sliced

1. Dissolve the gelatine in a little water. Combine the fromage blanc and cream. Add the gelatine to the cheese and whipped cream mixture.
2. Set in 4 small dessert rings for 2 hours.
3. Cook the sugar and 200 ml (7 fl oz) water until a light coloured caramel. Add the slices of candied ginger. Pour the caramel around the Bavarois.

ROUXL BRITANNIA
London, EC2

Tomato and Basil Soup
Cod Fillet with a Parsley and Garlic Crust
Apple and Banana Crumble

Serves 4–6

Tomato and Basil Soup

6–8 basil leaves
100 g (4 oz) butter
1 medium onion, skinned
  and roughly chopped
1 clove of garlic, skinned
  and finely chopped
400 g (14 oz) tomatoes,
  roughly chopped

50 ml (2 fl oz) white wine
500 ml (17 fl oz) vegetable
  stock or water
7.5 ml (½ tbsp) tomato
  purée
salt and pepper
double cream, to serve

1. Chop the basil leaves and stalks, leaving a couple of the leaves
   for garnish, also chopped.
2. Place the butter in a saucepan and heat gently. Sweat the onion
   and garlic in the saucepan, without colouring. Add the chopped
   tomatoes and basil, and cook for a couple of minutes.
3. Stir in the white wine, vegetable stock and tomato purée. Bring
   to the boil, then allow to simmer for 15–20 minutes.
4. Purée the contents of the pan in a blender. Pass through a
   strainer to remove any seeds and skins. Return the soup to the
   rinsed out pan, reheat, taste and season.
5. Place the soup into soup bowls and garnish with the chopped
   basil and a little twirl of double cream.

Note: This soup can also be served chilled.

Cod Fillet with a Parsley and Garlic Crust

100–150 g (4–5 oz) white
  breadcrumbs
2–3 cloves of garlic, skinned
  and finely chopped
50 g (2 oz) finely chopped
  fresh parsley
olive oil
four or six 100–150 g
  (4–5 oz) cod fillets
75–100 g (3–4 oz) butter
salt and pepper

Beurre blanc sauce:
20 ml (4tsp) white wine
  vinegar
2 shallots, skinned and
  finely chopped
100 ml (4 fl oz) white wine
10 white peppercorns,
  crushed
200 ml (7 fl oz) double
  cream
150 g (5 oz) butter

1. For the crust, place the white breadcrumbs, garlic and parsley in a food processor or blender. Mix together, adding enough olive oil to make it a little moist.
2. Check the cod fillets to make sure there are no bones. Meanwhile place the butter in a saucepan and gently melt. Season the cod fillets and dip into the melted butter, then into the crust mix, making sure you only dip or cover the top side of the fillet and not both sides.
3. Place the fillets on to a greased baking sheet. Cook in the oven at 200°C (400°F) mark 6 for about 6–8 minutes. Remove from the oven and place the fillets under the grill to colour the crust, only until golden brown. Keep warm.
4. For the sauce, put the white wine vinegar, shallots, white wine and crushed white peppercorns in a small saucepan. Bring to the boil and reduce by two-thirds. Add the cream, lower the heat and reduce until the cream has nearly doubled in thickness. Remove the pan from the heat and, using a wire whisk, mix in the butter a little at a time in quick succession. Taste and season. Pass through a strainer and serve immediately.
5. To serve, place the cod fillet in the centre of a main course plate surrounded by the beurre blanc sauce. Serve with new potatoes and spring vegetables.

Apple and Banana Crumble

3–4 Bramley apples
juice of ½ lemon
3–4 bananas
25 g (1 oz) butter
50 g (2 oz) caster sugar
4 cloves
pinch of ground cinnamon
icing sugar, for dusting

Crumble:
100 g (4 oz) demerara sugar
100 g (4 oz) butter
200 g (7 oz) plain flour

1. Peel, core, and roughly chop the apples and place immediately in a bowl of water with the lemon juice to avoid discolouring. Meanwhile, peel and roughly chop the bananas.
2. Place the butter in a saucepan and heat. Add the bananas, apples, caster sugar, cloves and a pinch of cinnamon. Mix together, lower the heat, cover and cook gently for 5–6 minutes. Make sure that the fruit are still in rough pieces and not broken down.
3. Meanwhile for the crumble mix, combine all the ingredients together.
4. Remove the fruit mixture from the saucepan and divide into 4–6 portions in individual ramekins or place in a large ovenproof dish. Cover the fruit with the crumble mix and pat down firmly.
5. Cook the crumble in the oven at 200°C (400°F) mark 6 for about 10–12 minutes or until the crumble mix has turned to a dark golden brown colour. Sprinkle with icing sugar and serve hot with custard or cream.

RSJ
London, SE1

Vegetable and Herb Tart with Curry Sabayon
Stuffed Chicken Legs
Chocolate Mousse

Serves 4–6

Vegetable and Herb Tart with Curry Sabayon

1 medium onion, skinned
1 small carrot, peeled
50 g (2 oz) fennel
50 g (2 oz) leek, washed
2 sticks of celery
25 g (1 oz) sorrel
25 g (1 oz) fresh spinach
50 g (2 oz) broccoli
1 small courgette
30 ml (2 tbsp) olive oil
1 small clove of garlic,
    skinned and crushed
1 bay leaf
15 ml (1 tbsp) chopped
    fresh tarragon

30 ml (2 tbsp) chopped
    fresh herbs, chervil, dill
    and chives
300 ml (½ pint) double
    cream
salt and pepper
1 large baked pastry case

Curry sabayon:
50 ml (2 fl oz) white wine
50 ml (2 fl oz) wine vinegar
10 ml (2 tsp) curry powder
2 egg yolks
450 ml (¾ pint) clarified
    butter
salt and pepper

1. Chop all the vegetables and keep separate. In a large saucepan, heat the olive oil and garlic and cook for 30 seconds, without colouring.
2. Add the vegetables and herbs in the order listed at about 30 second intervals, with the courgette last. Add the cream. Bring to the boil for 1 minute and check the seasoning.
3. Spread the mixture on to a deep tray and allow to cool until needed.
4. Place the white wine, vinegar and curry powder in a bowl and combine. Add the egg yolks and place over a pan of hot water. Whisk until thickened, then remove from the heat.

5. Gradually pour in a third of the clarified butter. Whisk, then add the rest of the butter. Whisk gently. Season to taste.
6. Place the vegetable filling into the pastry case, top with curry sabayon and glaze under the grill. Serve with a crisp salad.

Stuffed Chicken Legs

1 shallot, skinned and
  chopped
1 clove of garlic, skinned
  and crushed
butter and oil for cooking
225 g (8 oz) sausage meat
25 g (1 oz) dried apricots,
  chopped

15 ml (1 tbsp) mixed
  chopped fresh herbs
salt and pepper
25 g (1 oz) toasted flaked
  almonds
4 boned chicken legs

1. Sweat the shallot and garlic in a little butter and oil, then allow to cool. Place the sausage meat in to a bowl and mix with a wooden spoon. Thoroughly mix in the apricots, chopped herbs, shallot, garlic, salt and pepper and flaked almonds.
2. Open out the boned chicken legs and fill with the stuffing, reshape and tie with string.
3. In a frying pan with oil and butter, add the legs and brown all over. Roast in the oven at 220°C (425°F) mark 7 for 15–20 minutes or until cooked. Serve with rice and a cream sauce.

Chocolate Mousse

150 g (5 oz) dark chocolate
50 g (2 oz) egg white
75 g (3 oz) caster sugar
1½ leaves of gelatine, soaked
  in cold water

30 ml (2 tbsp) dark rum
15 ml (1 tbsp) grated
  chocolate

1. Place the dark chocolate in a small bowl. Stand in a warm place and allow to melt.
2. Beat the egg white and sugar in a mixer until quite stiff. Melt the soaked gelatine in the dark rum and pour into the egg mixture while still beating on fast speed.
3. Pour in the melted chocolate and mix in thoroughly. Remove from the machine and fold in the grated chocolate. Chill in the refrigerator overnight.

LES SAVEURS
London, W1

Chestnut Cream Soup
Roast Salmon with Herb Vinaigrette
Lime Soufflé

Serves 4

Chestnut Cream Soup

**300 g (11 oz) shelled
chestnuts**
**500 ml (18 fl oz) chicken
stock**
200 ml (7 fl oz) cream
100 ml (4 fl oz) truffle juice
100 ml (4 fl oz) truffle oil
**200 g (7 oz) duck liver,
trimmed and chopped**

**20 g (¾ oz) fresh truffles
(optional)**
salt and pepper
**100 ml (4 fl oz) top of the
milk**
chervil, to garnish

1. Cook the chestnuts in the chicken stock. Add the cream and, when boiling, stir in the truffle juice and truffle oil.
2. Pan fry the duck liver. Stir into the soup and, if you can afford them, the fresh truffles. Add salt, pepper and the top of the milk. Garnish with chervil.

The crab
off

Roast Salmon with Herb Vinaigrette

4 salmon steaks, about
  150 g (5 oz) each

Vinaigrette:
200 ml (7 fl oz) olive oil
30 ml (2 tbsp) sherry
30 ml (2 tbsp) balsamic
  vinegar

20 ml (4 tsp) honey
100 g (4 oz) tomato,
  chopped
100 g (4 oz) artichoke,
  chopped
chopped fresh basil,
  tarragon and chervil
salt

1. Pan fry the salmon in very hot olive oil; cook on the skin side only.
2. Put the salmon in a dish with some olive oil. Cook in the oven at 130°C (250°F) mark ½ for about 10 minutes.
3. Combine the vinaigrette ingredients. Serve the salmon with the vinaigrette and new potatoes.

Lime Soufflé

4 egg yolks
100 g (4 oz) caster sugar,
  plus extra for coating
40 g (1½ oz) custard powder
750 ml (1¼ pints) milk,
  boiled

6–8 limes
100 g (4 oz) egg white
200 ml (7 fl oz) double
  cream
50 g (2 oz) butter
100 g (4 oz) honey

1. Beat the egg yolks and sugar together. Stir in the custard powder and boiled milk. Add the juice of 4 limes and the grated zest of 2.
2. Whisk the egg whites until stiff and fold into the mixture with the cream.
3. Coat a soufflé dish with butter and sugar and add the soufflé mixture. Cook in the oven at 220°C (425°F) mark 7 for about 8–10 minutes.
4. To make a sauce to serve with the soufflé, combine the honey and 10 ml (4 fl oz) lime juice in a pan. Serve the soufflé immediately.

SIMPSON'S-IN-THE-STRAND
London, WC2

London Particular
Lancashire Hot Pot
Treacle Roll

Serves 4

London Particular

1 carrot, peeled and
chopped
1 onion, skinned and
chopped
bouquet garni using bay leaf,
thyme, peppercorns,
parsley

225 g (8 oz) split green peas
1.1 litres (2 pints) chicken
stock
salt and pepper
croûtons, to serve

1. Boil all the ingredients together in a pan until the peas are soft.
   Remove the bouquet garni.
2. Purée in a blender, then pass through a strainer.
3. Correct the consistency, if necessary. Season. Serve with
   croûtons.

Lancashire Hot Pot

4 pieces middle neck of lamb	**1 onion, skinned and sliced**
oil for frying	**1 kg (2 lb) potatoes, peeled and sliced**
salt and pepper	

1. Remove the meat and long bone from the main neck bone. Chop the lamb into cutlets.
2. Make a stock from the discarded bones and trimmings.
3. Seal the meat in hot fat and arrange in the bottom of an oven-proof dish. Season with salt and pepper. Cover with a layer of onion. Cover completely with overlapping potato slices.
4. Add stock to the level of the potatoes. Cook in the oven at 170–180°C (325–350°F) mark 3–4 for about 1½ hours or until the meat is tender. Serve in the dish.

Treacle Roll

225 g (8 oz) self-raising flour	**50 g (2 oz) sugar**
225 g (8 oz) beef suet	**100 g (4 oz) golden syrup**
1 egg	

1. To make suet pastry, rub the flour and suet together. Add the egg and sugar and enough water to make a smooth dough. Roll out the dough into a rectangular shape. Fold the edges over.
2. Spread the syrup over the dough, then roll up into a cylinder shape. Place onto a tray and cover with greased greaseproof paper.
3. Steam for 1½–2 hours. Serve with custard.

SLOANS
Birmingham

Carrot and Coriander Soup
Chicken Tagliatelle with ham and mushrooms
Crème Brûlée

Serves 4–6

Carrot and Coriander Soup

¼ bunch of fresh coriander
700 g (1½ lb) carrots,
    peeled and chopped
450 g (1 lb) onions, skinned
    and sliced
oil for cooking

1.1 litres (2 pints) chicken
    stock
600 ml (1 pint) milk
cream, to garnish

1. Remove the coriander leaves from the stalks. Sweat the carrots and onions together in a little oil with the coriander stalks for 5 minutes.
2. Add the hot chicken stock and simmer until the carrot is soft.
3. Reserve a little of the coriander leaves to chop for garnish. Add the rest of the soup followed by the milk. Bring to the boil. Purée in a blender, then pass through a sieve.
4. Finish with a little cream and reserved the chopped coriander.

Chicken Tagliatelle with ham and mushrooms

4 chicken supreme, cut into
    0.5 cm (¼ inch) dice
4 slices of Bayonne ham, cut
    into strips
oil and butter for cooking
200 g (7 oz) button
    mushrooms
150 ml (¼ pint) chicken stock

900 ml (1½ pints) double
    cream
150 g (5 oz) button onions,
    skinned and blanched
salt and pepper
chopped fresh coriander and
    basil, to garnish

1. Sauté the diced chicken and ham in a little oil, then drain. Cook the mushrooms in butter.
2. Reduce the chicken stock by three-quarters, then add the cream. Reduce again by half, then add the button mushrooms, onions and chicken and ham. Season.
3. Toss the freshly cooked noodles in a little butter. Place in a bowl and spoon over the chicken mixture. Sprinkle with coriander and basil to serve.

Noodle Paste
500 grms strong flour
2 packets saffron powder

5 whole eggs
seasoning
olive oil

1. Add the saffron eggs, salt and pepper and enough olive oil to the flour to gradually bind to a paste. Beat the paste for 5 minutes.
2. Rest the noodle paste for 2 hours before using.
3. Cut into tagliatelle and cook in salted water.

Crème Brûlée

1 vanilla pod, split in half lengthwise
900 ml (1½ pints) double cream or half each double and single cream

8 egg yolks, size 1 or 2
50 g (2 oz) caster sugar
caster sugar for topping

1. Place the split vanilla pod into the cream in a pan and bring to the boil. Boil for about 30 seconds.
2. Beat the egg yolks and sugar together. Pour the cream onto the egg and sugar mixture. Return the mixture to the saucepan and cook over a low heat or in a bain marie until it thickens and coats the back of a spoon.
3. Remove the vanilla pod, pour the cream into 4 ramekins, and chill. Before serving, sprinkle the cream with an even layer of caster sugar and place in an iced bain marie under a preheated grill at maximum temperature to caramelise the sugar.

SMITH'S
London, WC2

Watercress and Cheddar Salad
Pot Roast Knuckle of Bacon
Apple and Coconut Crumble

Serves 4–6

Watercress and Cheddar Salad

1 bunch of watercress per
   person, trimmed and
   washed
50 g (2 oz) Montgomery
   Cheddar cheese per
   person, shaved

Dressing:
salt and pepper
pinch of sugar
1 clove of garlic, skinned
   and crushed
lemon juice
5 ml (1 tsp) Dijon mustard
100 ml (4 fl oz) light olive
   oil

1. Mix the salt, pepper and sugar with the garlic and lemon juice until the ingredients have come together. Stir in the mustard and olive oil.
2. Toss the watercress and cheese together in a salad bowl with the dressing.

Pot Roast Knuckle of Bacon

4–6 knuckles of bacon
15–30 ml (1–2 tbsp) oil
3 cloves of garlic, skinned
  and crushed
2 onions, skinned and finely
  diced
2 leeks, washed and sliced
sprig of thyme
chopped fresh parsley
sage leaves

350–450 g (12 oz–1 lb)
  lentils (de Puy)
3 sweet potatoes, peeled and
  sliced
4 carrots, peeled and sliced
1 turnip, peeled and
  chopped into quarters
salt and pepper
1 savoy cabbage, cut into
  thick lengths, to serve

1. Soak the knuckles overnight in cold water. Wash the knuckles and bring to the boil in 600 ml (1 pint) fresh water.
2. Heat the oil in a flameproof casserole and cook the garlic, onions, leeks and herbs over a gentle heat until caramelised. Add the knuckles and cooking stock.
3. Cover and cook in the oven at 150°C (300°F) mark 2 for 50 minutes. Add the lentils, sweet potatoes, carrots, turnip and seasoning. Cook for a further 25 minutes. Return the casserole to the stove and steam the cabbage for a further 10 minutes.
4. Remove the knuckle, serve with the lentils, carrots and sweet potatoes. Add the cabbage to the plate and serve with the juices. Garnish with chopped parsley.

Today
Fishermans
pie

Apple and Coconut Crumble

9 large eating apples,
  peeled, cored and
  chopped
175 g (6 oz) granulated
  sugar
juice of 1 lemon
butter

Crumble:
225 g (8 oz) plain flour
225 g (8 oz) butter
100 g (4 oz) desiccated
  coconut
225 g (8 oz) granulated
  sugar

Custard:
600 ml (1 pint) milk
1 vanilla pod
3 egg yolks
100 g (4 oz) caster sugar

1. Place the apples, sugar, lemon juice and 150 ml (¼ pint) water in a pan and gently cook until the apples are soft.
2. For the crumble, mix the flour, butter, coconut and sugar together with your fingers until all the ingredients 'crumble' through your fingers.
3. Pour the apple compote into a baking dish and cover with the crumble mix. Sprinkle with sugar and add a few dabs of butter. Cook in the oven at 150°C (300°F) mark 2 for 25–30 minutes.
4. For the custard, heat the milk with the vanilla pod and bring to the boil. Whisk the egg yolks and sugar until pale, then stir into the mixture. Return to the saucepan, continually stirring. Cook over a gentle heat until the custard coats the back of a wooden spoon. Pass through a fine sieve. Serve the custard with the crumble.

SMOLLENSKY'S BALLOON
London, W1, WC2

Herbed Split Pea Soup
Pork Fillet with Barbecue Sauce
Dutch Rum Apple Cake

Serves 4–6

Herbed Split Pea Soup

450 g (1 lb) dried green
  split peas
2.3 litres (4 pints) unsalted
  chicken stock, preferably
  homemade
225 g (8 oz) smoked ham,
  chopped
4 cloves of garlic, skinned
  and crushed

1 sprig of fresh parsley
2 bay leaves
2.5 ml (½ tsp) dried thyme
2.5 ml (½ tsp) dried
  marjoram
4 whole cloves
2 medium onions, skinned
  and halved
salt

1. In a stockpot, combine the split peas, chicken stock, ham, garlic and herbs. Stick a clove into each piece of onion and add to the soup.
2. Bring to the boil over a high heat. Immediately reduce the heat to low, partially cover and simmer until the peas have just about disintegrated and can be mashed against the side of the pot with a fork, about 2 hours.
3. Taste the soup and season to taste with salt and additional herbs, as desired. Purée in a food processor or blender. Reheat and serve.

Pork Fillet with Barbecue Sauce

225 g (8 oz) fillet of pork
oil for frying

Barbecue sauce:
60 ml (4 tbsp) butter
60 ml (4 tbsp) vinegar
60 ml (4 tbsp) chilli sauce
60 ml (4 tbsp) lemon juice
60 ml (4 tbsp)
Worcestershire sauce

1 clove of garlic, skinned
and crushed
1 medium onion, skinned
and chopped
dash of cayenne
dash of Tabasco sauce
2.5 ml (½ tsp) salt
2.5 ml (½ tsp) pepper

1. For the barbecue sauce, in a small saucepan melt the butter. Mix in all the other ingredients. Simmer for a few minutes.
2. Butterfly the pork steak and fry for 4 minutes on each side. Cover with barbecue sauce and simmer for 2 minutes. Serve with freshly prepared French fries.

Dutch Rum Apple Cake

Pastry:
300 g (11 oz) plain flour
165 g (5½ oz) butter, cut
  into flakes
165 g (5½ oz) caster sugar
2 egg yolks
pinch of salt

Filling:
450 g (1 lb) cooking apples,
  peeled, cored and sliced

30 ml (2 tbsp) rum
75 g (3 oz) caster sugar
juice of 1 lemon
pinch of ground cinnamon
50 g (2 oz) raisins
50 g (2 oz) ground almonds

Icing:
30 ml (2 tbsp) cream cheese
75 g (3 oz) icing sugar,
  sifted

1. For the pastry, sift the flour into a bowl and rub in the butter. Stir in the sugar, egg yolks and salt and mix quickly to a dough. Wrap in foil or cling film and leave for 2 hours in the refrigerator.
2. Roll out just over half the pastry to line a 25 cm (10 inch) loose-bottomed flan tin. Bake blind in the oven at 200°C (400°F) mark 6 for 15 minutes.
3. For the filling, mix the apples with the rum, sugar, lemon juice, cinnamon, raisins and ground almonds. Moisten with water to blend. Spoon into the pastry case and smooth over.
4. Roll out the remaining pastry to cover the filling and seal the edges together well. Bake for a further 30 minutes, then cool in the tin overnight.
5. For the icing, mix the cream cheese and icing sugar together. Spread over the top of the cake.

SNOWS ON THE GREEN
London, W6

Tomato and Pistou Soup
Pan-Fried Sardines with Tapenade Toast
Stewed Fruit Compote

Serves 4

Tomato and Pistou Soup

Plum tomatoes provide the best flavour.

Pistou:
1 large bunch of basil
4 cloves of garlic
4 tomatoes, skinned, seeded and diced (plum if possible)
5 ml (1 tsp) grated Parmesan cheese
salt and pepper
250 ml (8 fl oz) extra virgin olive oil

Soup:
100 ml (4 fl oz) virgin olive oil

1 onion, skinned and finely chopped
2 cloves of garlic, skinned and finely chopped
12 plum tomatoes, seeded and diced
15 ml (1 tbsp) caster sugar
600 ml (1 pint) vegetable or chicken stock (or water)
4 slices of stale bread, roughly chopped
15 ml (1 tbsp) grated Parmesan cheese
salt and pepper

1. To make the pistou, put all the ingredients, except the olive oil, in a blender. Rather like making mayonnaise, add the olive oil very slowly, keeping the blender on, until you have a smooth paste no thinner than double cream.
2. For the soup, combine the oil, onion and garlic in a saucepan and sauté until the onion is transparent, without browning. (At this stage it will be very oily.)

3. Next add the tomatoes and cook for 5 minutes before adding the sugar, which will remove any bitterness in the tomatoes. Then add the stock and bring to the boil. The soup may seem very runny but adding the bread will soak up the excess liquid. Depending on how thick you like your soup, add more or less bread. Add the Parmesan and salt and pepper and simmer the soup slowly for a further 30 minutes.
4. If you want to serve the soup hot, pour it into 4 bowls and then put 15 ml (1 tbsp) pistou dressing on top. If you prefer to serve it cold, do the same but chill the soup thoroughly first.

Pan-fried Sardines with Tapenade Toast

8 sardines, backbones removed
clarified butter
1 ciabatta loaf, sliced into 8 pieces

Ratatouille:
olive oil
1 red onion, skinned and finely diced
2 cloves of garlic, skinned and crushed
1 aubergine, finely diced
2 courgettes, finely diced
2 green peppers, seeded and finely diced
2 yellow peppers, seeded and finely diced
2 red peppers, seeded and finely diced

5 ml (1 tsp) finely chopped fresh rosemary
5 ml (1 tsp) finely chopped fresh thyme
5 ml (1 tsp) finely chopped fresh flat parsley
2 tomatoes, skinned, seeded and diced
salt and pepper

Tapenade:
30 ml (2 tbsp) stoned black olives
4 anchovy fillets
15 ml (1 tbsp) capers
7.5 ml (½ tbsp) lemon juice
olive oil to blend

1. To make the ratatouille, heat olive oil in a pan and sauté the onion and garlic until soft. Add the aubergine, courgettes, peppers and herbs and continue cooking vigorously for 5 minutes.

Add the tomatoes, adjust the seasoning and cook for a further 2 minutes. Remove from the heat.

2. For the tapenade, mix all the ingredients together in a food processor, except the olive oil. Keeping the processor on slowly, add the olive oil until you have a smooth paste.

3. Lightly flour the sardines and sauté in clarified butter until golden brown. While the sardines are cooking, grill the slices of ciabatta and spread with the tapenade.

4. Put 2 pieces of toast on each plate, top with the reheated ratatouille and place the sardines on top. Finish with a little extra virgin olive oil over the top.

Stewed Fruit Compote

This is better made the day before and kept overnight in the refrigerator. Serve either piled high in a glass bowl or in individual dishes.

225 g (8 oz) caster sugar
1 cinnamon stick
1 vanilla pod
6 fennel seeds
6 whole cloves
1 pear, peeled and quartered
2 sticks of rhubarb, peeled and cut into 8 pieces
4 fresh figs
8 dried prunes
8 dried apricots
8 dried chestnuts
1 pink grapefruit, peeled and segmented
1 clementine, peeled and segmented
2 blood oranges, peeled and sliced
crème fraîche, to serve

1. Combine 600 ml (1 pint) water, the sugar, cinnamon, vanilla pod, fennel seeds and cloves in a saucepan and bring to the boil. Simmer for 30 minutes.

2. Cook the pear in the liquid for 4 minutes and remove with a slotted spoon, then the rhubarb for 3 minutes and remove, then the figs for 2 minutes and remove.

3. Cook all the dried fruits in the same liquid for 2 minutes and remove. Cool all the cooked fruit.

4. When cool, combine all cooked fruit with the citrus fruit. Strain the syrup and pour over. Serve with crème fraîche.

SONNY'S
London, SW13

Smoked Haddock and Gruyère Tart
Chicken, Chorizo and White Bean Casserole
Apple and Cranberry Crisp

Serves 4

Smoked Haddock and Gruyère Tart

Pastry:
275 g (10 oz) plain flour
225 g (8 oz) unsalted butter, cut into small pieces
5 ml (1 tsp) salt

Filling:
350 g (12 oz) smoked haddock (undyed), skinned

100 g (4 oz) Gruyère cheese, grated
225 g (8 oz) spinach, washed

Custard filling:
300 ml (½ pint) single whipping cream
2 eggs
salt and pepper

1. For the pastry, in a mixer blend the butter into the dry ingredients until the breadcrumb stage. Add 150 ml (¼ pint) cold water at once and mix further until a dough is formed. Rest the dough for 1 hour.
2. Roll out the pastry and line a 23 cm (9 inch) flan tin. Bake blind in the oven at 170°C (325°F) mark 3 for about 15 minutes.
3. Slice the haddock thinly. Cook the spinach in butter until wilted. Drain well and separate.
4. Layer the tart case, starting with Gruyère, sliced haddock, spinach, Gruyère, haddock and lastly Gruyère.
5. Mix the custard ingredients together and pour over the tart.
6. Bake in the oven at 190°C (375°F) mark 5 for about 40 minutes until set and coloured on top.

Chicken, Chorizo and White Bean Casserole

900 g (2 lb) boneless
  skinless chicken leg or
  breast, cut into 2.5 cm
  (1 inch) dice
15 ml (1 tbsp) vegetable oil
225 g (8 oz) chorizo
  sausage, sliced or diced

one 400 g (14 oz) can whole
  peeled plum tomatoes
100 g (4 oz) white beans,
  soaked and cooked
600 ml (1 pint) chicken
  stock
salt and pepper

1. Sauté the chicken in the oil until just seared. Sauté the chorizo until coloured. Set aside.
2. Crush the tomatoes in a flameproof casserole. Add the white beans, stock, chicken and chorizo.
3. Simmer until the stock is reduced and the chicken is cooked through. Season lightly as the chorizo can be quite spicy.
4. Serve with rice.

Apple and Cranberry Crisp

This is a wonderfully simple dessert which requires very little looking after. The resulting sweet crunchy texture of the topping offsets the sharp tart flavour of the soft fruit superbly. You can also serve the dish with thick crème fraîche.

Topping:
175 g (6 oz) walnuts,
  coarsely chopped
225 g (8 oz) flour
250 g (9 oz) demerara sugar
2.5 ml (½ tsp) ground
  cinnamon
pinch of salt
175 g (6 oz) unsalted butter,
  cut into small pieces and
  softened

Filling:
4 large Bramley apples,
  peeled, cored and sliced
100 g (4 oz) cranberries
25 g (1 oz) plain flour
100 g (4 oz) sugar

1. For the topping, mix all the ingredients together thoroughly.
2. Mix the filling ingredients together and put in a pie dish. Spread the crisp topping over the filling about 2.5 cm (1 inch) deep.
3. Bake in the oven at 200°C (400°F) mark 6 for about 45 minutes. Check that the fruit is cooked by skewering the filling.

STEPHEN BULL'S BISTRO
London, EC1

Apple and Beetroot Borscht
Cassoulet of Pork, Chorizo and Chick Peas
Coffee and Cardamom Crème Caramel

Serves 4–6

Apple and Beetroot Borscht

1 onion, skinned and finely chopped
2 sticks of celery, finely chopped
2 cloves of garlic, skinned and finely chopped
1 leek, washed and finely chopped
30 ml (2 tbsp) duck fat or lard
1.5 litres (2½ pints) chicken or duck stock
450 g (1 lb) cooked beetroot, grated
1 large cooking apple, peeled, cored and grated
juice of 1 lemon
30 ml (2 tbsp) white wine vinegar
salt and pepper
1 large pickled gherkin, finely chopped
soured cream or crème fraîche, to serve

1. Sweat the onion, celery, garlic and leek in the duck fat or lard.
2. Pour on the stock, bring to the boil and simmer for 10 minutes.
3. Add the beetroot, apple, lemon juice and vinegar. Simmer for 10 minutes. Season with salt and pepper.
4. Add the gherkin and a generous swirl of soured cream or crème fraîche. (Can be served hot or cold.)

Cassoulet of Pork, Chorizo and Chick Peas

1 kg (2 lb) boneless, rindless belly pork
25 g (1 oz) salt
25 g (1 oz) sugar
50 g (2 oz) duck or goose fat or lard
50 g (2 oz) Bayonne or Serrano ham or bacon, diced
1 onion, skinned and finely chopped
1 carrot, peeled and finely chopped
1 stick of celery, finely chopped
1 leek, washed and finely chopped
2 cloves of garlic, skinned and crushed
1 small turnip, peeled and finely chopped
15 ml (1 tbsp) herbes de Provence
30 ml (2 tbsp) tomato purée
250 g (9 oz) dried chick peas, soaked overnight
1.1 litres (2 pints) chicken stock
1 small chilli, finely chopped
2 confit legs chicken or duck, flaked (optional)
1 bay leaf
1 sprig of thyme
450 g (1 lb) chorizo sausage, sliced 1 cm (½ inch) thick
1 small spring cabbage, shredded
25 g (1 oz) chopped fresh parsley
grated zest and juice of 1 lemon
75 g (3 oz) breadcrumbs or brioche crumbs
salt and pepper

1. Cure the pork overnight in the salt and sugar. Wash the salt and sugar off the pork. Dice the meat into lean 1 cm (½ inch) cubes.
2. Melt the duck fat in large flameproof casserole. Sweat the pork and ham or bacon for 3 minutes. Add the onion, carrot, celery, leek, garlic, turnip and herbes de Provence and sweat for a further 10 minutes.
3. Add the tomato purée, then the chick peas and stock. Bring to the boil, skim all the scum from the top and simmer for 20 minutes.
4. Add the chilli and confit (optional), bay leaf, thyme, sausage and cabbage. Bring back to the boil, cover and cook in the oven at 190°C (375°F) mark 5 for about 20 minutes or until the meat is cooked.
5. Meanwhile, mix the parsley, lemon juice and grated zest, breadcrumbs, salt and pepper. Remove the cassoulet, sprinkle the breadcrumb mix over the top and put the lid back on. Cook until the chick peas are tender, about 20 minutes.

Coffee and Cardamom Crème Caramel

600 ml (1 pint) milk
4 cardamom pods, seeds
  finely crushed
10 ml (2 tsp) instant coffee
  granules

225 g (8 oz) sugar
4 eggs, size 3
flaked almonds, toasted, and
  orange segments, to
  decorate

1. Infuse the milk with cardamom and coffee over a gentle heat for 20 minutes.
2. For the caramel, place half the sugar in a pan and heat gently to caramelise.
3. Meanwhile, beat the eggs and sugar together well. Strain the milk over the egg mixture. Line 6 ramekins or 1 larger mould with the caramel sauce (use any excess as sauce later) and pour in the egg and milk mixture.
4. Bake in a bain marie in the oven at 150°C (300°F) mark 2 for 45–60 minutes. Cool and turn out. Decorate with orange segments and toasted almonds.

ST OLAVES COURT HOTEL
Exeter, Devon

Mussels with Garlic and Lemon
Stuffed Chicken Legs with a Yellow Lentil Purée
Rhubarb Crumble

Serves 4–6

Mussels with Garlic and Lemon

1 kg (2 lb) mussels, washed
  and prepared
300 ml (½ pint) fish stock
2 cloves of garlic, left whole
juice of 1 lemon

50 g (2 oz) chopped fresh
  parsley
300 ml (½ pint) double
  cream

1. Place the mussels in the saucepan with the fish stock, garlic, lemon juice and parsley. Cook to open the mussels; discard any which do not open.
2. Remove the opened mussels with a slotted spoon and place in a warmed serving dish. Keep warm.
3. Add the cream to the remaining juices in the pan and reduce by half to a good consistency. Pour over the mussels and serve immediately.

Stuffed Chicken Legs with a Yellow Lentil Purée

4 chicken legs, boned
225 g (8 oz) yellow lentils
unsalted butter
salt and pepper
4 potatoes, peeled

2 shallots, skinned and
  chopped
1 egg
300 ml (½ pint) double
  cream

Stuffing:
450 g (1 lb) mushrooms
1 chicken breast, skinned
  and chopped
50 g (2 oz) chopped fresh
  tarragon

Sauce:
50 g (2 oz) veal glace (veal
  stock reduce to solid when
  set)
300 ml (½ pint) chicken
  stock

1. For the stuffing, place the ingredients into a mixer and blend until smooth.
2. Stuff the chicken legs with the smooth mixture, drawing the skin back into a 'leg' shape and fix with wooden cocktail sticks. Cook in the oven at 200°C (400°F) mark 6 for 20–25 minutes until cooked.
3. While the chicken is cooking, stew the lentils in water for 20 minutes. When cooked, purée with plenty of unsalted butter and season to taste.
4. Cook and mash the potatoes, season with salt and pepper. Keep warm.
5. For the sauce, reduce the veal glace and chicken stock together to a good gravy consistency.
6. Arrange the mashed potato and lentils on warm plates. Place the chicken legs on top, after removing the cocktail sticks. Pour over the gravy and serve.

Rhubarb Crumble

700 g (1½ lb) fruit mixture,
  chosen from rhubarb,
  sultanas, raisins, pears,
  soaked dried apricots
ground cinnamon
soft brown sugar

Crumble topping:
100 g (4 oz) unsalted butter
225 g (8 oz) plain flour
50 g (2 oz) caster sugar

1. For the crumble topping, rub the butter into the flour and add the sugar, making a fine sandy texture.
2. Stew the fruit mixture with a little cinnamon and sugar to taste until soft. Put into individual ramekins. Cover the fruit with crumble topping and sprinkle with soft brown sugar.
3. Bake in the oven at 220°C (425°F) mark 7 for 10–15 minutes. Serve with crème fraîche.

LA TRUFFE NOIRE
London, SE1

Baked Goat's Cheese Toasts
Steaks with Roquefort Cheese
Melon Cups

Serves 4–6

Baked Goat's Cheese Toasts

salt and pepper
15 ml (1 tbsp) vinegar
45 ml (3 tbsp) walnut oil
15 walnuts
1 curly endive

6 Crottin de Chavignol or
similar small, soft goat's
cheeses
6 slices of bread

1. Dissolve a pinch of salt in the vinegar. Add the oil, walnuts and pepper to taste. Place in the bottom of a salad bowl and set aside.
2. Rinse and drain the endive. Separate the leaves. Add to the salad bowl but do not toss.
3. Cut a 1 cm (½ inch) slice from the base of each cheese. Reserve these slices for another recipe. Cut the cheeses in half.
4. Trim the slices of bread so they are just slightly larger than the cheeses. Place a halved cheese on each slice of bread.
5. Arrange the toasts on a baking sheet. Bake in the oven at 220°C (425°F) mark 7 for 8 minutes. Then grill the cheese toasts for 4–5 minutes, watching them carefully.
6. Toss the chicory with the dressing. Serve with the hot cheese toasts.

Steaks with Roquefort Cheese

75 g (3 oz) butter
50 g (2 oz) flour
1 litre (1¾ pints) hot milk
six 225 g (8 oz) boneless
   sirloin or entrecôte steaks

250 ml (8 fl oz) crème
   fraîche
225 g (8 oz) Roquefort
   cheese

1. Melt 50 g (2 oz) of the butter in a saucepan over a gentle heat. As soon as it begins to foam, add the flour and stir until completely absorbed. Add the milk and cook, stirring well, over a gentle heat for about 10 minutes.
2. Meanwhile, heat the remaining butter in a frying pan, add the steaks and cook for 3–5 minutes on each side.
3. Stir the crème fraîche into the sauce. Add two-thirds of the cheese and mix carefully.
4. Pour the sauce over the steaks. Crumble the rest of the cheese over the steaks and serve very hot.

Melon Cups

1 large cantaloupe melon
1 kg (2 lb) mixed fresh fruit,
   such as grapes, pears,
   strawberries, oranges
100 g (4 oz) sugar

60 ml (4 tbsp) Kirsch or
   maraschino liqueur
250 ml (8 fl oz) thick crème
   fraîche

1. Cut a lid off the melon and scoop out the fruit in balls using a ball-cutter or a teaspoon. Discard the seeds.
2. Wash the fresh fruit and peel, dice and remove seeds where necessary. Place the fruit in a bowl with the melon balls and sprinkle with the sugar and liqueur. Leave to steep in the refrigerator for 1 hour.
3. Just before serving, fill the melon shell with the fruit salad. Serve well chilled with the crème fraîche.

TURNER'S
London, SW3

Marinated Salmon with a Sweet Mustard Vinaigrette
Supreme of Corn Fed Chicken with Herbs
Crème Caramel

Serves 4

Marinated Salmon with a Sweet Mustard Vinaigrette

450–550 g (1–1¼ lb) filleted
  salmon
100 g (4 oz) coarse sea salt
100 g (4 oz) caster sugar
2 bunches of dill, chopped
juice of 1 orange
juice of 1 lime
50 ml (2 fl oz) Cognac
pepper
mixed salad leaves, to serve

Mustard vinaigrette:
200 ml (7 fl oz) stock syrup
100 ml (4 fl oz) white wine
  vinegar
2 eggs
½ bunch of dill, chopped
dash of Worcestershire
  sauce
10 ml (2 tsp) made mustard
dash of soy sauce
dash of Pernod (optional)

1. Combine the sea salt and sugar and cover the flesh side of the salmon completely with the mixture. Wrap in foil and leave in the refrigerator for 6 hours.
2. Wash away the salt and sugar completely and cover with chopped dill, orange and lime juice and Cognac. Wrap again in foil and press lightly. Leave to rest overnight before serving.
3. Cut into required portions and grill or pan-fry for 3 minutes. Place on bed of crisp salad leaves.
4. For the vinaigrette, combine the stock syrup, white wine vinegar, eggs, chopped dill, Worcestershire sauce, mustard and soy sauce in a food processor or blender. A dash of Pernod may also be added. Pour over the salmon.

Supreme of Corn-fed Chicken with Herbs

4 boneless corn fed chicken
  breasts, with skin
4 chicken legs, boned and
  without any sinew
1 bunch of basil, tarragon
  and parsley
salt and pepper
2 egg whites

175 ml (6 fl oz) double
  cream
2 shallots, skinned
butter for cooking
4 rashers of smoked bacon,
  chopped
1 savoy cabbage, chopped

1. Place the chicken breasts between cling film and, using a meat bat or rolling pin, beat lightly until about 2 cm (¾ inch) thick.
2. Place the meat from the legs in a blender and process until minced. Add the herbs, seasoning and egg whites and blend for 1 minute. Remove from the machine, add the cream slowly and mix with a wooden spoon. Allow to rest for 1 hour.
3. Place the breasts on foil and pipe or spoon the prepared chicken mousse along the flattened breast. Roll the foil into a sausage shape and twist at both ends to seal. Cook in the oven at 180°C (350°F) mark 4 for about 15 minutes, turning every 5 minutes to ensure that they emerge golden all over. Allow to rest for 5 minutes before serving.
4. Sweat the shallots in butter without colouring, then add the smoked bacon and cook lightly. Blanch the savoy cabbage. Add to the bacon and shallots. Slice the chicken sausage at an angle and serve on a bed of the cabbage and bacon mixture.

Crème Caramel

275 g (10 oz) sugar
400 ml (14 fl oz) single
  cream

4 egg yolks
2 vanilla pods

1. Bring 225 g (8 oz) of the sugar and 400 ml (16 fl oz) water to a caramel in a thick bottomed pan over a gentle heat. Pour the caramel into the bases of 4 ovenproof moulds.
2. Whisk the cream into the beaten egg yolks, the remaining sugar and the pith of the vanilla pods. Strain and pour the cream mixture into the moulds on top of the caramel.
3. Place the moulds in a roasting tin half full of warm water. Cook in the oven at 150°C (300°F) mark 2 for about 30 minutes. Press the tops lightly to check the custard is firm. Loosen the edges and turn out on to a flat dish, allowing the caramel to surround.

THE UBIQUITOUS CHIP
Glasgow

Spiced Pear Savoury with Soda Scones
Ayrshire Ham with Butter Beans, Buchan Style
Honey and Scotch Whisky Parfait

Serves 4–6

Spiced Pear Savoury with Soda Scones

3 soda scones or similar slices of good bread (Italian works well)
2 medium pears, peeled
2 chillies
6 black peppercorns
10 ml (2 tsp) demerara sugar
juice of ½ lemon
1 clove
good olive oil
bunch of watercress, washed and chopped
thick blue cheese sauce

Soda scones:
225 g (8 oz) self-raising flour
1.25 ml (¼ tsp) salt
2.5 ml (½ tsp) bicarbonate of soda
5 ml (1 tsp) cream of tartar
50 g (2 oz) margarine
milk to mix
egg to glaze

1. Put the pears into a pan and cover with water. Add the chillies, peppercorns, demerara sugar, lemon juice and one clove. Bring to the boil, reduce to simmer and cook until the pears are perfectly cooked but still retain a bite. Leave to cool in the liquor until required.

2. For the soda scones, sift the dry ingredients together. Rub in the margarine and add just enough milk to give a soft dough. Place on a lightly floured surface and roll out to 2.5 cm (1 inch) thick. Cut out 12 cm (5 inch) rounds and place on a well greased baking tray. Brush with egg. Cook in the oven at 230°C (450°F) mark 8 for 10 minutes.

3. Slice the scones horizontally and place cut side up. Brush around the edges with the olive oil. Place some watercress in the middle of each scone.

4. Drain and slice the spiced pears and put on top of the watercress. Top the pear slices with a good spoonful of blue cheese sauce.
5. Bake in the oven for a few minutes until the edges are crisp and the cheese takes on a little colour. Garnish with sprigs of watercress.

Ayrshire Ham with Butter Beans, Buchan Style

1.4–1.8 kg (3–4 lb) ham
450 g (1 lb) dried butter beans
15 ml (1 tbsp) demerara sugar
pinch of mace
black peppercorns
10 ml (2 tsp) honey
fresh brown breadcrumbs
cloves
watercress, to garnish

1. Soak the ham overnight in lots of cold water. Soak the beans overnight in lots of cold water.
2. Drain the ham, put in a pan and cover with fresh water. Add the sugar, mace and peppercorns and bring to the boil. Reduce the heat to a low simmer, cover and cook for 30 minutes per 450 g (1 lb) weight. Remove the ham and reserve the stock.
3. Drain the beans. Cook in the ham stock until tender. (This should take approximately 1½ hours but can vary with the age of the beans.)
4. Strip the skin from the ham, rub the exposed fat with honey, pat on fresh breadcrumbs and stick with the cloves. Heat in the oven at 190°C (375°F) mark 5 for about 30 minutes. Serve slices of ham on top of the warm beans. Garnish with lots of watercress.

Honey and Scotch Whisky Parfait

3 eggs
1 measure of Scotch Whisky
30 ml (2 tbsp) clear honey
150 ml (¼ pint) double cream

1. Separate the eggs and whisk the whites until stiff.
2. Warm the honey slightly until runny. Put the egg yolks in a mixer and very slowly beat in the honey followed by the Scotch. Whip the cream and fold into the beaten egg whites.
3. Divide the mixture between 6 ramekins and freeze. Remove from freezer approximately 10 minutes before required.

VERONICA'S
London, W2

Arbroath Smokies
Rumbledethumps
Whipkull

Serves 4

Arbroath Smokies

200 g (7 oz) Arbroath smokies, off the bone and roughly chopped
120 ml (4½ fl oz) double cream

20 ml (4 tsp) chopped chives
5 ml (1 tsp) cayenne
4 slices of granary bread

1. Mix the smokies and cream together in a pan. Heat gently.
2. Stir in the chopped chives. Sprinkle with cayenne. Serve with toasted granary bread, cut into rings.

Rumbledethumps

800 g (1 lb 12 oz) mashed
  potato
30 ml (2 tbsp) fried onion
50 g (2 oz) cooked spring
  greens
four 25 g (1 oz) cubes
  Dunlop cheese (similar to
  Cheddar)
50 g (2 oz) plain flour

1 egg, beaten
100 ml (4 fl oz) milk
200 g (7 oz) nibbed
  almonds
oil for deep frying
200 g (7 oz) Dunlop (or
  Cheddar) cheese
200 g (7 oz) dill pickle,
  to serve

1. Combine the mashed potato, fried onion and spring greens and divide into four.
2. Roll each portion around a cube of cheese, forming 4 balls in all with cheese in the centre. Then flatten to approximately a 10 cm (4 inch) circular patty.
3. Dip in order into the flour, beaten egg, milk and then into nibbed almonds. Heat the oil on medium setting to deep fry for about 5 minutes until golden brown.
4. Top with grated cheese. Allow to melt for a few seconds under a hot grill. Serve accompanied by dill pickles.

Whipkull

This foaming dessert is taken as a Christmas drink in the Shetlands – a custom shared with the Norwegians. It bears a passing resemblance to zabaglione.

3 eggs
3 egg yolks
75 g (3 oz) caster sugar

120 ml (4½ fl oz) dark rum
250 ml (8 fl oz) white wine

1. Whip all the ingredients together over a low heat (or in a double saucepan) until thick and frothy, about 2 minutes. Serve immediately accompanied by Highland shortbread.

VILLANDRY
London, W1

Spinach Soup
Italian Meat Loaf
Lemon Tart

Serves 4

Spinach Soup

900 g (2 lb) young spinach,
  washed
4 onions, skinned and sliced
50 g (2 oz) butter
2 cloves of garlic
salt and pepper
2 potatoes, roughly chopped
grated nutmeg
1.1 litres (2 pints) chicken
  or vegetable stock

Croûtons:
butter
8–12 slices of French bread,
  cut diagonally
sprinkling of fresh
  Parmesan cheese

1. Remove the stalks from the spinach.
2. Soften the onions in the butter, add the garlic and season with salt and pepper. Add the potatoes and spinach, stir until the spinach is wilted. Stir in some grated nutmeg and the stock.
3. Cook until the potatoes are soft.
4. Taste and adjust seasoning as necessary. Purée in a blender.
5. For the croûtons, put a pat of butter on each slice of bread and sprinkle with a pile of Parmesan. Put them under the grill until the Parmesan colours slightly. Serve hot with the soup.

Italian Meat Loaf

2 red peppers
olive oil
2 courgettes, diced
25 g (1 oz) butter
2 cloves of garlic, skinned
   and crushed
salt and pepper
handful of mushrooms,
   sliced
about 225 g (8 oz) new
   potatoes, scrubbed
1 large onion, skinned and
   finely diced

900 g (2 lb) best minced
   beef
25 g (1 oz) Gruyère cheese,
   grated
chopped fresh parsley
1 egg, size 1

Marinated red onions:
2 red onions, skinned and
   finely sliced
peppercorns
1 bay leaf
champagne vinegar

1. For the marinated red onions, place the onions in a sieve. Pour boiling water over.
2. Place the onions in a jar with a few peppercorns and a bay leaf. Cover the onions with a mixture of one third of champagne vinegar and two-thirds boiling water. Allow to marinate for at least 1 hour.
3. To roast the red peppers, place the peppers on a baking tray and rub with olive oil. Roast in the oven at medium heat until the skins are soft. Remove the peppers, place them in a plastic bag and allow to cool. (This makes it easier to remove their skins.) When cool, remove the skin, seeds and core; then dice the flesh.
4. Sauté the courgettes in butter with the garlic, and season with salt and pepper. Sauté the mushrooms.
5. Cook the new potatoes, peel and dice.
6. Soften the onion in butter and season with salt and pepper. Mix the onion, minced beef and Gruyère together in a bowl. Add some chopped parsley. Finally, add the egg to bind the ingredients together and season with salt and pepper.
7. Melt a little butter in a frying pan and cook a spoonful of the mince, taste and test for seasoning. Adjust the seasoning as necessary.
8. Lay a large sheet of greaseproof paper on top of a tea towel. Empty the bowl of mince on to the paper and beat it into an oblong shape about 1 cm (½ inch) thick. Sprinkle with chopped parsley.

9. Then spread a stripe of each filling onto the mince, so that it looks like a rainbow – with 1 stripe of courgettes, 1 stripe of mushrooms, 1 stripe of new potatoes and 1 stripe of red peppers (stripes, not layers).
10. Carefully roll up the mince (so that it resembles a Swiss roll) releasing the greaseproof paper as you go. Place the roll on a greased baking tray. Cook in the oven at 190–200°C (375–400°F) mark 5–6 for about 45 minutes or until cooked. Slice and serve with the marinated red onions.

Lemon Tart

Pastry:
175 g (6 oz) plain flour
50 g (2 oz) caster sugar
75 g (3 oz) unsalted butter
1 egg
vanilla essence
grated rind of 1 lemon

For the filling:
250 ml (8 fl oz) lemon juice, strained
175 g (6 oz) caster sugar
90 ml (6 tbsp) double cream
8 eggs
2 egg yolks
15 ml (1 tbsp) plain flour

1. For the pastry, mix the flour and sugar together in a bowl. Rub in the butter. Add the egg, a few drops of vanilla essence and lemon rind. Chill for 30 minutes.
2. Roll out the pastry to 3 mm (⅛ inch) thick and use to line a 30cm (12 inch) flan ring.
3. Bake blind in the oven at 170°C (325°F) mark 3 for 20 minutes until dry and light brown.
4. For the filling, mix the lemon juice and sugar together and mix in the cream. Beat in each egg separately and finally the yolks. Fold in the flour.
5. Pour into the baked pastry case. Reduce the oven temperature to 150°C (300°F) mark 2 and cook until set but not brown.

THE VINTNERS' ROOMS
Edinburgh

Marinated Salmon and Mackerel
Rabbit with Basil
Walnut Treacle Tart

Serves 6

Marinated Salmon and Mackerel

350 g (12 oz) salmon fillet, cut into thick fingers
350 g (12 oz) mackerel fillet, cut into thick fingers
salt
slices of avocado and fresh coriander leaves, to serve

Marinade:
75 ml (⅛ pint) orange juice
75 ml (⅛ pint) lemon juice
75 ml (⅛ pint) olive oil
4 thin slices of orange, cut into 4
½ red pepper, seeded and diced
1 shallot, skinned and finely sliced
salt and pepper

1. Fillet the fish and cut into appropriate sizes.
2. Place the fish in a flameproof dish, salt lightly and leave for 30 minutes.
3. Mix the marinade ingredients together and pour over the fish. Bring to the boil and cook for a few seconds. Let cool.
4. Serve with slices of avocado, coriander leaves and ginger rice.

Rabbit with Basil

1 rabbit, jointed
8 bacon rashers
25 g (1 oz) butter and oil for frying
1 sprig of fresh thyme, chopped
2 shallots, skinned and chopped
300 ml (½ pint) dry white wine

salt and pepper
150 ml (¼ pint) double cream
1 egg yolk
15 ml (1 tbsp) chopped fresh parsley
15 ml (1 tbsp) chopped fresh basil
10 ml (2 tsp) lemon juice

1. Wrap the rabbit joints in bacon, pinning with cocktail sticks. Heat the butter and oil in a flameproof casserole and fry the rabbit gently.
2. Sprinkle with fresh thyme and shallot, and pour over the wine. Season. Braise gently in the oven at 140°C (275°F) mark 1 for about 1 hour or until tender. Add about half of the double cream.
3. Remove the rabbit from the pan, remove the cocktail sticks and keep the rabbit warm. Sieve the sauce. Combine the egg yolk, remaining cream, parsley and basil. Add a spoonful of the egg and cream mixture to the hot sauce with the lemon juice. Stir in the remaining egg and cream mixture, pour the sauce over the rabbit and serve with pasta.

Note: Use farmed rabbit, unless wild known to be young.

Walnut Treacle Tart

1 baked sweet shortcrust pastry case

Filling:
100 g (4 oz) butter
100 g (4 oz) soft brown sugar

3 eggs
175 g (6 oz) golden syrup
225 g (8 oz) walnuts
juice and grated rind of 1 lemon
pinch of salt

1. Cream together the butter and sugar until light and smooth. Beat in the eggs, one at a time.
2. Warm the syrup slightly until runny and mix into the butter and sugar, with the nuts, lemon juice, rind and salt. Turn into the pastry case.
3. Bake in the oven at 200°C (400°F) mark 6 for about 30–45 minutes. Serve warm or cold with cream or a scoop of ice cream.

WALTON'S
London, SW3

Home Smoked Chicken with Apple and Pear Chutney
Baked Salmon and Scallop Tower
Chocolate Nut Pudding with Chocolate Sauce

Serves 4–6

Home Smoked Chicken with Apple and Pear Chutney

2 chicken breasts, with skin
oak shavings for smoke box
   (see page 107)
mixed salad leaves
salad dressing

Chutney:
50 g (2 oz) shallots, skinned
25 g (1 oz) butter
1 carrot, peeled and finely
   diced

2 sticks of celery, diced
1 mango, peeled and diced
2 apples, peeled, cored and
   diced
2 large pears, peeled, cored
   and diced
50 g (2 oz) honey
25 g (1 oz) fresh mint,
   chopped

1. For the chutney, cook the shallots in the butter until soft.
2. Add the carrot, celery and mango, then the apple, pear and honey. Cook until the fruit is soft.
3. Take off the heat and add the chopped mint.
4. Smoke the chicken breasts. Take out and slice lengthways. Arrange dressed salad leaves on plates, add strips of chicken and chutney. Serve with warm bread.

Baked Salmon and Scallop Tower

450 g (1 lb) salmon fillet
4 egg whites
600 ml (1 pint) double
  cream
25 g (1 oz) fresh dill,
  chopped
25 g (1 oz) fresh chervil,
  chopped
6 large scallops, diced
salt and pepper
225 g (8 oz) blanched
  spinach
50 g (2 oz) tomato, diced, to
  garnish

Sauce:
25 g (1 oz) shallot
4 tomatoes, chopped
25 g (1 oz) butter
150 ml (¼ pint) dry white
  wine
300 ml (½ pint) fish stock
300 ml (½ pint) double
  cream
pinch of saffron

1. Purée the salmon in a food processor. Add the egg whites slowly, then the double cream.
2. Place the mixture in a bowl. Add the chopped herbs and diced scallops. Correct seasoning.
3. Pipe into individual buttered moulds, layering with the spinach. Cover with foil. Bake in a bain marie in the oven at 200°C (400°F) mark 6 for 20 minutes.
4. For the sauce, cook the shallot and tomatoes in the butter. Add the white wine and reduce. Add the fish stock and reduce.
5. Stir in the double cream and saffron, bring to the boil, then correct the seasoning. Strain and serve.
6. Turn out the moulds onto plates and pour the sauce around. Garnish with herbs and tomatoes.

Chocolate Nut Pudding with Chocolate Sauce

100 g (4 oz) butter
75 g (3 oz) sugar
4 eggs, separated
50 g (2 oz) walnuts,
chopped
100 g (4 oz) digestive
biscuits, chopped
100 g (4 oz) dark chocolate,
chopped

Chocolate sauce:
225 g (8 oz) sugar
40 g (1½ oz) cocoa powder
15 ml (1 tbsp) cornflour
pinch of salt
50 g (2 oz) dark chocolate

1. Cream the butter and 50 g (2 oz) of the sugar, then add the egg yolks.
2. Crush the walnuts, biscuits and chocolate in a food processor, then stir into the egg and sugar mixture.
3. Whisk the egg whites and remaining sugar, then fold in last.
4. Butter 6 individual ramekins and place a piece of greaseproof paper on the bottom. Pour in the mixture and cover each ramekin with foil. Place in a bain marie and cover the bain marie with foil. Cook in the oven at 170°C (325°F) mark 3 for 40 minutes.
5. Meanwhile for the chocolate sauce, in a heavy bottomed pan boil 175 ml (6 fl oz) water and 100 g (4 oz) of the sugar until the sugar has dissolved. Add the cocoa powder, cornflour, salt and 120 ml (4 fl oz) water to the mixture and thicken. Add the dark chocolate and remaining sugar. Stir until a good thickness and serve with the pudding.

WHEELER'S
see Restaurant List for locations

Wheeler's Fish Soup
Wheeler's Salmon Kedgeree
Poached Peaches with Caramel Sauce

Serves 6

Wheeler's Fish Soup

1 small onion, skinned
25 g (1 oz) leek (white only)
25 g (1 oz) fennel
25 g (1 oz) celery
1 clove of garlic, skinned
  and crushed
olive oil
1.4–1.7 litres (2½–3 pints)
  fish stock

25 g (1 oz) tomato purée
2 tomatoes, chopped
150 ml (¼ pint) white wine
pinch of saffron
250 g (9 oz) mixed selection
  of prepared fish pieces
  and shellfish
garlic croûtons, to serve
  (optional)

1. Cut the vegetables into very small dice. Fry lightly with the garlic in olive oil.
2. Add the stock, tomato purée, tomatoes, wine and saffron. Bring to the boil and skim. Simmer for 20–30 minutes.
3. Warm the fish and shellfish selection, cooking if necessary, and put in the bottom of soup bowls. Pour on the soup. Garnish with garlic croûtons if required.

Wheeler's Salmon Kedgeree

350 g (12 oz) salmon
150 ml (¼ pint) dry white
   wine
2 small onions, skinned and
   chopped
1 carrot, peeled and sliced
1 stick of celery, chopped
15 ml (1 tbsp) lemon juice
6 peppercorns
1 bouquet garni

salt and pepper
350 g (12 oz) long grain rice
50 g (2 oz) butter
7.5 ml (1½ tsp) English
   mustard powder
3 eggs, hard–boiled and
   quartered
cayenne pepper
celery leaves or parsley
   sprigs, to garnish

1. Put the salmon in a saucepan, pour in the wine and enough water to cover the fish. Add half of the chopped onions, the carrot, celery, lemon juice, peppercorns, bouquet garni and 5 ml (1 tsp) salt.
2. Bring slowly to the boil, then remove from the heat. Cover tightly and cool.
3. Cook the rice in a saucepan of boiling salted water for 15–20 minutes until tender.
4. Meanwhile, remove the salmon from the liquid and flake the fish, discarding skin and any bones. Strain the cooking liquid and reserve.
5. Melt half of the butter in a large frying pan, add the remaining onion and fry gently until soft. Drain the rice thoroughly, then add to the onion with the remaining butter. Toss gently to coat in the butter and stir in the mustard powder.
6. Add the flaked salmon and hard-boiled eggs with a few spoonfuls of the strained cooking liquid to moisten. Heat through. Shake the pan and toss the ingredients gently so that the salmon and eggs do not break up.
7. Transfer to a warm serving dish and sprinkle with cayenne pepper to taste. Serve immediately, garnished with celery leaves or parsley.

Poached Peaches with Caramel Sauce

6 ripe peaches

Syrup:
275 g (10 oz) sugar
**1 vanilla pod or 15 ml
  (1 tbsp) vanilla sugar**
rind of ½ lemon
juice of 1 lemon

Caramel sauce:
175 g (6 oz) caster sugar
15 ml (1 tbsp) honey
**300 ml (½ pint) single
  cream**
50 g (2 oz) unsalted butter

1. Simmer all the syrup ingredients together with 1.7 litres (3 pints) water for 30 minutes.
2. Skin the peaches by pouring boiling water over them first. Cook the peaches in the syrup for 20–30 minutes.
3. For the caramel sauce, put the sugar in a saucepan with 50 ml (2 fl oz) water. Cook until caramelised. Remove from the heat and cool slightly.
4. Add the honey, single cream and butter and whisk together. Allow to cool.
5. Drain the peaches from the syrup and serve cool on top of the caramel sauce.

WILLOUGHBY'S
London, N1

Lettuce Soup

Cawl

Baked Bay Custard

Serves 6

Lettuce Soup

This is a variation on watercress soup. It was served hot in January but could be served cold in the summer.

2 small or 1 large onion(s), skinned and chopped	**1.4 litres (2½ pints) vegetable stock or water**
20 g (¾ oz) butter	**salt and pepper**
700 g (1½ lb) lettuce, chopped	**90 ml (6 tbsp) cream, to serve**
1 kg (2¼ lb) potatoes, peeled and diced	**chopped fresh mint or parsley, to garnish**

1. Sweat the onion in the butter in a large saucepan for 5 minutes, without browning.
2. Add the lettuce and potatoes and cook gently for 5–10 minutes, stirring occasionally. Do not allow the vegetables to brown.
3. Stir in the stock or water, cover the pan and simmer for 20 minutes until the potatoes are tender. Season to taste, then purée in a blender. Pour 15 ml (1 tbsp) cream into bowls before adding the soup. Garnish with chopped herbs.

Cawl

This traditional Welsh dish is sometimes served using lamb only, but is better with two meats.

sunflower oil
350 g (12 oz) shin of beef
550 g (1¼ lb) best end neck
  of lamb
1 large onion, skinned and
  thickly sliced
2 carrots, peeled and sliced
1 small swede or turnip,
  peeled and cut up
450 g (1 lb) potatoes,
  scrubbed

1 stick of celery, sliced
bouquet garni
sprig of thyme
1 small white cabbage,
  sliced
2 small leeks, washed and
  sliced
salt and pepper
chopped fresh parsley

1. Heat the oil in a pan and brown the meats whole. Transfer to a flameproof casserole. Fry the root vegetables in the pan, then transfer to the casserole.
2. Add the celery, bouquet garni and thyme, then enough water to come to within about 5 cm (2 inches) below the rim of the casserole. Bring slowly to a simmer, removing any scum as it appears. Simmer, uncovered, for about 4 hours. Add hot water if necessary.
3. Add the cabbage and leeks after 3¾ hours. Season to taste, cut up the meats, remove the bouquet garni and add chopped parsley to serve. Serve with good bread.

Baked Bay Custard

450 ml (¾ pint) milk
150 ml (¼ pint) whipping or
  double cream
6 bay leaves (dried have
  more flavour, fresh look
  more attractive)

4 eggs
100 g (4 oz) caster sugar

1. Bring the milk and cream to the boil with the bay leaves. Leave to stand for 15 minutes.
2. Meanwhile, whisk the eggs and sugar together until pale and frothy. Strain the milk and cream into the eggs, stirring constantly. Pour the mixture into 6 ramekins and put a bay leaf in each.
3. Transfer the ramekins to a bain marie. Cover and bake in the oven at 170°C (325°F) mark 3 for about 45 minutes.
4. Remove the custards, allow to cool and chill before serving.

ZOE
London, W1

Bruschetta of Marinated Mushrooms and Grilled Leeks
Corn Cakes Topped with Smoked Chicken Salad
Vanilla Croissant Pudding with Whisky Sauce

Serves 4–6

Bruschetta of Marinated Mushrooms and Grilled Leeks

450 g (1 lb) field
   mushrooms
90 ml (6 tbsp) extra virgin
   olive oil
2.5 ml (½ tsp) sesame oil
2 cloves of garlic, skinned
   and halved
40 ml (2½ tbsp) Chardonnay
   wine

30 ml (2 tbsp) chopped
   fresh coriander
salt and pepper
12 baby leeks
bay leaves
orange juice flavoured
   melted butter
slices of country bread
slices of Mozzarella

1. Wipe the mushrooms with a damp cloth. Heat the oil in a large frying pan and stir in the garlic; cook until soft but not brown. Add the mushrooms and turn them over in the oil. Cover the pan and cook over a low heat for about 7 minutes.
2. Transfer the mushrooms to a shallow dish with the garlic. Add the wine to the pan and boil the liquid fast for 5 minutes. Remove from the heat and allow to cool. Gradually stir in the coriander, seasoning and extra olive oil if required. Pour the mixture over the mushrooms.
3. Marinate the mushrooms for 2–3 hours or overnight. Steam the leeks over bay leaves for 8 minutes. Dip in olive oil and chargrill on both sides for 3 minutes. Dribble over the citrus butter.
4. Serve the mushrooms and grilled leeks on a slice of chargrilled country bread with a slice of Mozzarella. Heat in the oven or under the grill to melt the Mozzarella. Dribble with truffle or olive oil before serving.

Corn Cakes Topped with Smoked Chicken Salad

Corn cakes:
3 corn on the cobs, to produce about 250 g (9 oz) kernels
300 ml (½ pint) milk
225 g (8 oz) polenta
7.5 ml (1½ tsp) baking powder
2.5 ml (½ tsp) salt
15 ml (1 tbsp) honey
2 eggs, separated
75 ml (3 fl oz) vegetable oil
salt and pepper
clarified butter

Salad:
450 g (1 lb) smoked chicken meat, cut into julienne strips
225 g (8 oz) lobster meat, cut into medallions, or use diced claw (optional)
4 heads of chicory, cut into julienne strips
4 spring onions, trimmed and finely sliced
50 g (2 oz) walnuts, coarsely chopped
salt and pepper
30 ml (2 tbsp) balsamic vinegar
15 ml (1 tbsp) lemon juice
65 ml (2½ fl oz) walnut oil
60 ml (4 tbsp) gremolata (see page 87)
chopped chives, to garnish

1. For the cakes, work 150 g (5 oz) corn kernels with the milk in a blender for 4 minutes.
2. Pass the mixture through a mouli, leaving husks behind; resulting in a maximum of 300 ml (½ pint) liquid; do not use more.
3. Sift together the polenta, baking powder and salt. Add the honey, egg yolks and vegetable oil. Beating gently, add the corn milk, little by little, until the mixture is smooth. Stir in the remainder of the corn; season.
4. Brush a griddle or non–stick pan with clarified butter and heat gently. Meanwhile, whisk the egg whites to soft peaks and fold into the batter.
5. Pour 90 ml (6 tbsp) batter into a 10 cm (4 inch) metal ring sitting on the griddle. Cook for about 2 minutes over a medium heat until the bottom of the cake is set and the top has small bubbles. Flip over and cook for 90 seconds on the other side. Repeat to make 9 more pancakes.

6. For the salad, mix the chicken, lobster if using, chicory, spring onions and walnuts together; season.
7. Mix the vinegar, lemon juice and walnut oil together. Toss the salad ingredients gently with the dressing. Serve the salad on the corn cakes and garnish with chopped chives.

Vanilla Croissant Pudding with Whisky Sauce

Croissant pudding:
5 croissants, sliced and buttered
75 g (3 oz) raisins, soaked in whisky and water
3 eggs
2 egg yolks
600 ml (1 pint) milk
150 ml (¼ pint) double cream

100 g (4 oz) caster sugar
5 ml (1 tsp) vanilla essence

Whisky sauce:
100 g (4 oz) unsalted butter
100 g (4 oz) soft brown sugar
100 g (4 oz) caster sugar
1 egg
75 ml (5 tbsp) whisky

1. Place the slices of buttered croissant overlapping in a rectangular baking dish. Sprinkle over the raisins.
2. Combine the eggs and egg yolks in a large bowl: beat them lightly. In a saucepan, heat the milk, cream and sugar. Bring to a simmer, stirring to dissolve the sugar.
3. Add this to the egg mixture, whisking constantly. Add the vanilla and strain the mixture over the croissant slices. With a fork, press down on the croissants to ensure they absorb the custard.
4. Place the baking dish in a large pan of hot water. Bake in the oven at 180°C (350°F) mark 4 for about 45–50 minutes until the custard is brown on the top. A knife should come out clean.
5. For the sauce, melt the butter with both sugars in a saucepan over a low heat, stirring until the sugar is dissolved. Whisk the egg in another bowl and gradually fold in some of the melted butter mixture.
6. Fold this back into the melted butter pan and whisk over a low heat until smooth, about 1 minute; do not boil. Whisk in the whisky. Serve the croissant pudding with the whisky sauce.

A–Z RESTAURANT LIST

Increasingly, restaurants are staying open longer and later to combat rising overheads and to satisfy their customers' changing eating habits. Here is an alphabetical list of all the restaurants who have contributed recipes together with their address, telephone number and the times when they are closed.

1. **Adlard's Restaurant**, 79, Upper St. Giles Street, Norwich NR2 1AB, Tel 0603–633522. Closed Sat L, Sun and Mon.
2. **Alastair Little**, 49, Frith Street, London W1V 5TE, Tel 071–734 5183. Closed Sat L and Sun.
3. **The Argyll**, 316, Kings Road, London SW3 5UH, Tel 071–352 0025. Closed Mon L and Sun D.
4. **Au Jardin des Gourmets**, 5, Greek Street, London W1V 5LA. Tel 071–437 1816. Closed Sat L and Mon.
5. **Bahn Thai**, 21a, Frith Street, London W1V 5TS, Tel 071–437 8504. Open all week.
6. **Beauchamp's**, 25, Leadenhall Market, London EC3V 1LR, Tel 071–621 1331. Open Mon–Fri Lunch only.
7. **Belgo**, 72, Chalk Farm Road, London NW1 8AN, Tel 071–267 0718. Open all week.
8. **La Belle Epoque**, 61–3, Dublin Road, Belfast, Northern Ireland, Tel 0232–323244. Closed Sat L and Sun.
9. **Boyd's**, 135, Kensington Church Street, London W8 7LP, Tel 071–727 5452. Closed Sunday.
10. **The Brackenbury**, 129–131, Brackenbury Road, London W6 OBQ, Tel 081–748 0107. Closed Sat and Mon L, Sun D.
11. **Brasserie du Marché aux Puces**, 349, Portobello Road, London W10 5SA, Tel 081–968 5828. Closed Sun D.
12. **Brasserie Forty Four**, 42–44, The Calls, Leeds LS2 8AQ, Tel 0532–343232. Closed Sat L and Sun.
13. **Le Café des Amis du Vin**, 11–14, Hanover Place, Covent Garden, London WC2, Tel 071–379 3444. Closed Sun.
14. **Café des Arts**, 82, Hampstead High Street, London NW3, Tel 071–435 3608. Open all week.
15. **Café Flo Group**. Branches in Richmond, Surrey (081–940 8298), Fulham Road SW6 (071–371 9673), Islington N1 (071–226 7916), Kensington Church Street W8 (071–727 8142), Hampstead NW3 (071–435 6744) and St. Martins Lane WC2 (071–836 8289). Open all week.

16. **Café Royal Brasserie**, 68, Regent Street, London W1R 6EL, Tel 071–437 9090. Closed Sun D.
17. **Café Rouge Group**. Branches in SE1 (071–378 0097), Richmond, Surrey (081–332 2423), Wimbledon (081–944 5131), Kings Road SW3 (071–352 2226), Lancer Square W8 (071–938 4200), in Whiteleys W2 (071–221 1509), Putney SW15 (081–788 4257), James Street W1 (071–487 4847), Fulham Road SW3 (071–371 7600), Highgate (081–342 9797), Hampstead (071–433 3404), and Kensington Park Road W11 (071–221 4449). Open all week.
18. **Dan's**, 119, Sydney Street, London SW3 6NR, Tel 071–352 2718. Closed Sat L and Sun.
19. **Del Buongustaio**, 283, Putney Bridge Road, London SW15 2PT, Tel 081–780 9361. Closed Sat L.
20. **dell'Ugo**, 56, Frith Street, London W1V 5TA, Tel 071–734 8300. Closed Sat L and Sun.
21. **Frederick's**, Camden Passage, London N1 8EG, Tel 071–359 2888. Closed Sun.
22. **Gilbert's**, 2, Exhibition Road, London SW7 2HF, Tel 071–589 8947. Closed Sat L and Sun.
23. **Grill St Quentin**, 243, Brompton Road, London SW3 2EP, Tel 071–589 8005. Open all week.
24. **Hilaire**, 68, Old Brompton Road, London SW7 3LQ, Tel 071–584 7601. Closed Sat L and Sun.
25. **Le Marché Noir**, 2/4, Eyre Place, Edinburgh EH3 5EP, Tel 031–558 1608. Closed Sat and Sun at lunch.
26. **Markwicks**, 43, Corn Street, Bristol BS1 1HT, Tel 0272–262658. Closed Sat and Sun.
27. **The Marsh Goose**, High Street, Moreton in Marsh, Gloucestershire GL56 0AX, Tel 0608 52111. Closed Sun D.
28. **Le Mesurier**, 113, Old Street, EC1V 9JR, Tel 071–251 8117. Open Mon–Fri lunch only.
29. **Ming**, 35–36, Greek Street, London W1V 5LN, Tel 071–734 2721. Closed Sun.
30. **Newton's**, 33, Abbeville Road, South Side, Clapham Common, London SW4 9LA, Tel 081–673 0977. Open all week.
31. **Normandie**, Elbut Lane, Birtle, Nr Bury BL9 6UT, Tel 061–764 3869. Closed Sat L, Sun and Mon L.
32. **Odette's**, 130, Regent's Park Road, London NW1 8XL, Tel 071–586 5486. Closed Sat L and Sun D.
33. **Bistro 190**, 189 Queen's Gate, London SW7 5EU, Tel 071–581 5666. Open all week.
34. **192**, 192, Kensington Park Road, London W11 2ES, Tel 071–229 0482. Open all week.
35. **Osteria Antica Bologna**, 23, Northcote Road, London SW11 1NG, Tel 071–978 4771. Closed Mon and Tues L.

36. **Pomegranates**, 94, Grosvenor Road, London SW1V 3LF, Tel 071–828 6560. Closed Sat L and Sun.
37. **Ransome's Dock**, 35–37, Parkgate Road, Battersea, London SW11 4NP, Tel 071–223 1611. Closed Sun D.
38. **The Red Fort**, 77, Dean Street, London W1V 5HA, Tel 071–437 2115. Open all week.
39. **Restaurant and Arts Bar**, Jason Court, 76, Wigmore Street, London W1, Tel 071–224 2992. Closed Sun.
40. **Riva**, 169, Church Road, London SW13 9HR. Tel 081–748 0434. Closed Sat L.
41. **La Rive Gauche**, 61, The Cut, London SE1 8LL, Tel 071–928 8645. Closed Sat L and Sun.
42. **Rouxl Britannia**, Triton Court, 14, Finsbury Square, London EC2A 1RR, Tel 071–256 6997. Closed Sat and Sun.
43. **RSJ**, 13A, Coin Street, London SE1 8YQ, Tel 071–928 4554. Closed Sat L and Sun.
44. **Les Saveurs**, 37A, Curzon Street, London W1Y 8EY, Tel 071–491 8919. Closed Sat and Sun.
45. **Simpson's–in–the–Strand**, London WC2R OEW, Tel 071–836 9112. Open all week.
46. **Sloans**, 27–29, Chad Square, Hawthorne Road, Edgbaston, Birmingham B15 3TQ, Tel 021–455 6697. Closed Sat L and Sun.
47. **Smith's 5–7**, Neal Street, London WC2H 9PU, Tel 071–379 0310. Closed Sat L and Sun.
48. **Smollensky's Balloon**, 1, Dover Street, London W1X 3PJ, Tel 071–491 1199. Open all week.
49. **Smollensky's on the Strand**, 105, The Strand, London WC2R 0AA, Tel 071–497 2101. Open all week.
50. **Snows on the Green**, 166, Shepherds Bush Road, Brook Green, London W6 7PB, Tel 071–603 2142. Closed Sat L and Sun D.
51. **Sonny's**, 94, Church Road, Barnes, London SW13 0DQ, Tel 081–748 0393. Closed Sun D.
52. **Stephen Bull's Bistro**, 71, St John Street, London EC1M 4AN, Tel 071–490 1750. Closed Sat L and Sun.
53. **St. Olaves Court Hotel**, Mary Arches Street, Exeter, Devon EX4 3AZ, Tel 0392–217736. Closed Sat L.
54. **La Truffe Noire**, 29, Tooley Street, London SE1 2QF, Tel 071–378 0621. Closed Sat L and Sun.
55. **Turner's**, 87/89, Walton Street, London SW3 2HP, Tel 071–584 4441. Closed Sat L.
56. **The Ubiquitous Chip**, 12, Ashton Lane, Glasgow GL12 8SJ, Tel 041–334 5007. Open all week.
57. **Veronica's**, 3, Hereford Road, London W2 4AA, Tel 071–229 5079. Closed Sat L and Sun.

58. **Villandry**, 89, Marylebone High Street, London W1M 3DE, Tel 071–487 3816. Mon–Fri Lunch only.
59. **The Vintners' Rooms**, The Vaults, 87, Giles Street, Leith, Edinburgh EH6 6BZ, Tel 031–554 6767. Closed Sun.
60. **Walton's**, 121, Walton Street, London, SW3 2HP, Tel 071–584 0204. Open all week.
61. **Wheeler's**, 125, Chancery Lane, London W2, Tel 071–404 6071. Other branches at South Molton Street W1 (071–629 2471), Dover Street W1 (071–629 5417), Kensington High Street W8 (071–937 1443), Great Tower Street EC3 (071–626 3685), Fenchurch Street EC2 (071–606 8254), Duke Street W1 (071–930 2460) and Old Compton Street W1 (071–437 2706).
62. **Willoughby's**, 26, Penton Street, London N1 9PS, Tel 071–833 1380. Closed Sat L and Sun.
63. **Zoe**, 3–5, Barratt Street, London, W1, Tel 071–224 1122. Closed Sun.

Index

WIN A WEEKEND AT ONE OF THE UK'S TOP COUNTRY HOUSE HOTELS

A Weekend at Gidleigh Park –
Home to Chef Shaun Hill voted 'Chef of the Year 1993'

HOW TO ENTER

You are to host a dinner for six with no culinary restrictions and a total budget of £30. It is to be a creative, three-course menu with three bottles of wine (different or the same).

What will your menu be and which wines will you choose?

Menu	*Price*	
Starter	(£	)
Main Course	(£	)
Dessert	(£	)
Total cost		

Wines	*Price*	
1.	(£	)
2.	(£	)
3.	(£	)
Total cost		

Prize Draw Rules

1. There is one prize of a weekend for two at Gidleigh Park, Chagford, Devon to be awarded to the person whose menu is chosen. The weekend is to be taken between October 1994 and March 1995. The prize will exclude lunch and drinks. A cash alternative will not be offered.

2. The closing date for entries will be 30 April 1994. The winner will be announced by June 15 1994.

3. Entries lost, delayed or damaged in the post cannot be accepted. Proof of posting cannot be accepted as proof of delivery.

4. Entry is only open to residents of the United Kingdom, (aged 18 and over). Employees of the Financial Times and Random House and its associated companies, advertising agencies, printers and immediate families are not eligible to take part.

5. No correspondence will be entered into concerning this competition.

6. The name of the winner will be available from June 15 1994 by sending a self-addressed and stamped envelope to: Gidleigh Park Competition, Vermilion, Random House, London SW1V 2SA.